JN133107

Wilson in Okinawa
ウィルソン 沖縄の旅　1917

Tomoko Furui
古居 智子

序文

　ハーバード大学アーノルド樹木園の資料室でウィルソンが日本で撮った写真に出会って以来、撮影現場を特定し環境変化を考察するというのが私のライフワークになった。そして屋久島、鹿児島と続けた旅の先には、沖縄があった。

　「戦争で激変した沖縄で、100年前の風景を探しだすのは難しい」という意見が多くの人の口から発せられた。立ち止まった私の背中を押し、前に一歩踏み出す勇気を与えてくれたのは、同樹木園のウィリアム・フリードマン園長だった。

　「大きく変わってしまっているとしても、その事実をウィルソンの写真を通して伝えるのは大変意味深いことではないか」

　私の沖縄の旅は2016年2月から始まった。山や丘の稜線や海岸線を手掛かりに歩き回り、地域の人々から聞き取りを行い、また古い文献から撮影場所を推定していった。ウィルソンが記録した地名は、耳から聞いた単語をアルファベットに書き写しているため判断に迷うこともあった。例えば、"Shatan"が北谷のことであり、"Katena"が勘手納港ではなくて嘉手納町であることを確信するまでずいぶんと回り道をした。全部で59枚の写真のうち、予想をはるかに超える44枚の撮影場所を特定できた。私以上に熱心に、昔の面影を見つけて下さった各地の"ウチナーンチュ"の皆さんのご協力に支えられた結果であるのは言うまでもない。

　ウィルソンが「琉球の誉れ」と讃えたリュウキュウマツの大木は戦争と松食い虫の被害で数が減ってしまっていた。現在は街路、公園や墓地にコバテイシ（モモタマナ）の姿が目立つ。コバテイシは「人の泣き声を聞いて大きくなる」、と読谷で出会ったハーメー（おばあさん）が教えてくれた。ウィルソンの来沖から1世紀、その間に沖縄を襲った荒波とその余波を思う時、この言葉は胸に迫るものがあった。

　「100年後に記録に残す」という強い思いに裏付けされたウィルソンの写真は、失われた記憶との対話を促している。

Preface

　Ever Since I first encountered Wilson's photographs in the archive at Harvard University's Arnold Arboretum, identifying the locations and studying the environmental changes has become my lifework. After Yakushima and Kagoshima, this journey continued on to Okinawa.

　Many people voiced the opinion that, "After the upheaval of the war in Okinawa, tracking down scenes is going to be difficult." But I heard another voice; "Don't you think Wilson's photographs are profoundly meaningful as a medium to convey these changes?"

　My journey through Okinawa began in February, 2016. As I walked about I took clues from mountains and knolls and shorelines, interviewed the locals, and guessed photograph locations based on old literature. There were times when I had difficulty figuring out the place names recorded by Wilson, because these were names he had heard and then transcribed into roman characters. Out of a total of 59 photographs, I finally exceeded my expectations and identified the location of 44 photographs. I can't stress enough how much this result owes to the cooperation of all the Okinawans who uncovered vestiges of the past with passion surpassing my own.

　The Ryukyu Pines that Wilson called the "glory of Ryukyu" have dwindled as they have fallen victim to war and pine wilt nematodes. Today Sea Almond, which are said to grow large when they hear people crying, is conspicuous. This fact stirred in my heart whenever I thought of the hardships that Okinawa has endured and the aftermath of those struggles. Wilson's photographs embody his strong desire to leave a record that would remain one hundred years later and kindle the discussion of lost memories.

目次　Contents

序文　Preface …… 2
ウィルソンの琉球探訪
Wilson's Expedition to Ryukyu …… 4
Scene1　那覇　Naha …… 6
Scene2　奥武山　Onoyama …… 22
Scene3　宜野湾・嘉手納・読谷　Ginowan／Kadena／Yomitan …… 38
Scene4　慶良間諸島　Kerama Islands …… 48
Scene5　首里・中城　Shuri／Nakagusuku …… 58
Scene6　名護　Nago …… 68
Scene7　屋我地　Yagaji …… 78
Scene8　島人と植物　Island Life …… 88

もうひとつの物語 - ウィルソンと琉球を歩いた男
Another Story - The Man Who Walked with Wilson …… 100
ウィルソンの沖縄踏査地図
Wilson's Route in Okinawa …… 104
100年後のために記録に残す
Records for 100 Years Later …… 106
チーム・ウィルソン　Team Wilson …… 108
後記　Author's Note／謝辞　Acknowledgements …… 110
主な参考文献　References …… 111
著者紹介　Author's Profile …… 112

E.H.Wilson Photographs
© President and Fellows of Harvard College Arnold Arboretum Archive.
ウィルソンの写真提供：ハーバード大学アーノルド樹木園

ウィルソンの琉球探訪

　アーネスト・ヘンリー・ウィルソンは1876年、かつては羊毛業で栄えたイギリス中西部の小さな村、チッピング・カムデンに6人兄弟の長男として生まれた。家計を助けるために、小学校卒業と同時に園芸店に働き始めたのが植物に興味をもつきっかけとなった。3年後にバーミンガム植物園の庭師見習いの職を得ると、夜学校で植物学の基礎を身につけた。そして、21歳になった時には首都ロンドンにある世界有数の植物研究施設、キュー王立植物園に雇われるまでになった。

Ernest Henry Wilson
（1876-1930）

　そこで彼を待っていたのは、種苗会社の依頼で新種の植物を求めて中国奥地を探検する仕事だった。イギリスをはじめヨーロッパでは特に富裕層のあいだで園芸熱が盛んで、異国の新しい植物の移入は大きな利益をもたらした。若干23歳の若者は、たった一人で旅立ち、見事に幻の花「ハンカチノキ」（*Davidia involucrate*）の種子を持ち帰る。以来、通算4回の中国探検をことごとく成功させ、"伝説のプラント・ハンター"としての栄光の階段を一気に登りつめた。

　しかし最後の探検で崖崩れに遭遇し、右脚に障害が残る傷を負った。アメリカに居を移し、ハーバード大学アーノルド樹木園で植物分類の仕事や執筆業に専念するが、ウィルソンの本領はやはりフィールドワークにあった。そこで、園長の理解を得て企画されたのが日本への植物調査旅行だった。

　当時、日清日露の戦争で勝利を収めた日本は列強に追いつくために、国をあげて近代化の道を推し進めていた。1914（大正3）年、ウィルソンは鉄道と蒸気船を使って、屋久島をかわきりに北海道、サハリンまで旅をした。屋久島では周囲15.2mの大きな屋久杉の切株を発見し、その名を残したことで知られる。「ウィルソ

Wilson's Expedition to Ryukyu

　Ernest Henry Wilson was born the oldest of six children in 1876 in Chipping Campden, a small town in midwest England. He took an interest in plants when, after elementary school, he started working at a nursery to help the family's financial situation. Three years later, he gained employment as an apprentice at the Birmingham Botanical Garden and learned the fundamentals of botany at night school. At the age of 21, he was employed by the Royal Botanic Gardens, Kew, the world-leading botanical institute in London.

　The work he found there was an expedition to the interior of China in pursuit of new species of plants. At the time, England was at the head of a horticultural frenzy. As a young man, hardly 23 years old, Wilson succeeded in bringing back seeds of the rare handkerchief tree (*Davida involucrate*). He later embarked on a total of three more successful missions to China and leapt to the height of glory as the "legendary plant hunter."

　However, in his final expedition he met with a landslide, and suffered a life-threatening injury to his right leg. He moved to America, becoming absorbed in writing and work classifying plants at Harvard University's Arnold Arboretum, but it was fieldwork that was his specialty. So, a botanical survey trip to Japan was arranged.

　At the time, Japan, having achieved victory in the War with China and Russia, was pressing forward with mass modernization to catch up to major world powers. In 1914 Wilson traveled across all of mainland Japan using railway and steamship from Yakushima to Hokkaido and on to Sakhalin. In Yakushima, he discovered the ancient

ン株」と名付けられたこの切株は、現在は屋久島のシンボルとも言える観光スポットとなっている。

　7月、北海道を探検中に第一次世界大戦が勃発、帰国命令が発せられた。やむなく翌年初めにアメリカに戻るが、この1年間で撮影した写真は773枚、集めた植物標本はわかっているだけでも2千点近くにのぼる。

　2年後の1917年の年明け、ヨーロッパを主な戦場とする戦争が日々泥沼化の様相を示すなか、ウィルソンは周囲の反対を押し切って再び日本の地を踏んだ。当時大日本帝国の領土であった朝鮮半島、台湾にも足を延ばしている。この2回目の来日で、横浜に上陸したウィルソンが真っ先に目指したのは沖縄だった。鹿児島港を発った大阪商船会社の蒸気船は2日かけて鎖のように弧を描く島々を南下していった。

　ちょうど100年前の2月25日日曜日の朝のことだった。ウィルソンを乗せた蒸気船は狭い港口を通って貨物の積み下ろしで賑わう沖縄の玄関口、那覇港に舳を進めていた。人口6万人ほどの那覇区に近づくにつれ、黒々と繁茂する沖縄の固有種、リュウキュウマツの姿が目に飛び込んできた。

　「丘の上、墓に覆われた傾斜地、道路脇といった沖縄のあらゆるところで印象的な姿をしたマツを見た。これほど素晴らしい景観の島はかつて訪れたことがない」

　桜島を臨む薩摩の海岸で見かけて以来、自生する姿を一目見たいと願っていたリュウキュウマツが林立する姿を前に、ウィルソンは喜びの声をあげた。明るい陽光を浴びて、マツは下生えのシュロ、木性シダやソテツの上に影を落とし、見事なコントラストで風景に陰影を与えていた。

　南国の春は駆け足でやってくる。樹木の緑が濃くなり、草花は彩りを増し、耕地では田植えに勤しむ人影があった。亜熱帯の植物が潤いに満ちた風を受けて、独特の芳香を放っている。沖縄の島々は、「うりずん」と呼ばれる美しい季節を迎えていた。

cedar stump that measured 15.2m in girth, and he is remembered for this. Now, "Wilson Stump" is a major tourist destination, symbolic of Yakushima.

　Due to the outbreak of World WarⅠ, he was ordered to return to Boston early in the next year with 773 photographs and at least 2000 specimens.

　Two years later, at the beginning of 1917, as the war that claimed Europe as its main battleground seemed to drag on day after day, Wilson set out a second time to Japan despite the opposition of those around him and headed straight for Okinawa. It was the morning of Sunday, February 25, 100 years ago. The steamship passed through the narrow harbor entrance and steered its bow into port at Naha. As he drew near the port district with its population of 60,000, the dark luxuriant figures of Ryukyu Pines enticed the eyes of Wilson. "Pinus Luchuensis is everywhere with the striking feature in the landscape, on the hill-tops, slopes over graves and alongside the roads. I do not think I have visited a prettier land."

　Since catching sight of them in Kagoshima three years earlier Wilson had fervently hoped to see the figures of Ryukyu Pines growing wild, and now, with a thick stand of them before him, Wilson cried out in joy. Basking in bright sunlight, these Pines cast shadows upon the underbrush of Tree Ferns, Palms, Cycas and gave the splendid contrast of shade to the landscape.

　Springs comes fast to southern lands. The greens of trees and shrubs darken, flowering plants expand the palette, and the figures of workers planting rice can be seen in arable lands. The subtropical vegetation receives winds full of moisture and release unique fragrances. The islands of Okinawa were welcoming the beautiful season called, "Urizun."

Scene 1　那覇　Naha

島のすべての植生は基本的に常緑樹で、景色はとてもいい。
"The vegetation of all the islands is essentially evergreen, the scenery is pleasing."
E.H.Wilson

戦争に背を向けて
Leaving War Behind

「沖縄島の南端の西海岸にあり人口が集中する那覇は繁華な港町である。那覇港は琉球列島の主港で、蒸気船が荷物の積み下ろしのため埠頭に係留されていた」と、ウィルソンは走り書きのメモにつづっている。

明治時代になって火車（ヒイグルマ）と呼ばれる蒸気船が出入りするようになると、那覇港では本格的な湾岸工事が始まり、大正初めには大型船舶3隻が係留できる桟橋が完成した。かつては伝馬船が荷役を担っていた黒砂糖の樽は、軽便鉄道の引き込み線や荷馬車で汽船に運び込まれるようになり、遠く異国に向かう移民団を見送る人々もこの桟橋から手を振った。

Wilson scrawled in his notes, "Naha a thriving port of many inhabitants is situated near the southern end and on the west coast of Okinawa, the main island of the Liukiu group. Naha is the most important port in the group and steamers of good size come alongside a good wharf to load and unload."

At the port of Naha, coastal works had begun in earnest in the 19th century, and the wharf with moorings for three large ships was completed in early 20th century. Crates of brown sugar that used to be loaded by boats were now carried to steamships by wagon, unloaded from the light railway, as people waved farewell from the wharf to the emigrants bound for

当時は、いまだ自治権が制約された特別区制のもとにあったが、各地からの船が錨を下ろす商都那覇では活発な経済活動や文化活動が営まれ始めていた。港から大門前通りに抜ける目抜き道路には県庁、銀行をはじめ各種店舗が軒を並べ、ビアホールや映画館、劇場なども誕生し、娯楽を求める人々で賑わった。

　実はこの時、港の喧騒から少し距離を置いて漫湖沿岸の海岸植物群落に目を向けるウィルソンの胸中には、ヨーロッパを主戦場とした第一次世界大戦の影が付きまとっていた。その時の苦しい胸の内を綴った手紙が残されている。

　「長い時間をかけて熟考した結論ですが、私は平和が宣言されるまでアメリカには帰るつもりはありません。森の中にひとりでいる方が幸せですし、いい仕事ができると考えます」

　戦いの前線は塹壕戦のあげく膠着状態に陥り、先が見えなかった。ヨーロッパを二つに分断する軍民一体の総力戦が繰り広げられ、毒ガス、戦車、爆撃機、潜水艦といった最新兵器が次々と投入された。ウィルソンの故郷イギリス本土もドイツ軍の空襲を受け、子供を含む民間人の命が多数犠牲になっていた。

　「恐ろしい戦争が平和を破壊し、暮らしから安らぎと喜びを奪っています」

　当初は脚の障害のため兵士に志願できない身を呪っていたウィルソンだが、この頃にはすっかり厭世的になり、絶望の中に身を置くようになっていた。

　瓦屋根と茅葺屋根が混在する家々、黒々とした陰影を投げかけるリュウキュウマツ、そして背景に広がる港の風景。戦争に背を向け、南国の島にやってきたウィルソンの眼には、そのすべてが心癒される風景であったに違いない。

far-off countries.

　Although at that time Naha was still under a special administrative system with limited autonomy, ships from all over dropped anchor at this port city, which was alive with economic and cultural activity.

　However, for Wilson—who had his eyes on the coastal plant ecology of Manko, located a short distance from the hustle and bustle of the port—World War I cast a dark shadow on his heart, which followed him around as it claimed Europe as its main battleground. Some of this inner torment can be felt in his letters.

　"I have thought over this matter long and seriously and I have no desire to return to America, for I am happier here and can do better work in the woods and alone."

　The battlefront fell into the gridlock of trench warfare with no foreseeable way forward. As the all-out war of military and civilian personnel that divided Europe into two factions unfolded, poison gas, tanks, bombers, submarines, and other new weapons were introduced one after another. Wilson's home, England, was bombed by German forces, and countless civilians including children lost their lives.

　"This terrible war has ruined the art of peace and taken the contentment and pleasure out of life."

　Wilson, who could not apply to serve because of his leg injury, turned deeply pessimistic and found himself enveloped in despair.

　The intermingling of houses with tiled and thatched roofs, the deep black shadows of Ryukyu Pines, and the harbor scenery extending out in the background—surely all of these things must have calmed the heart of Wilson as he turned his back on the war, having arrived in these southern islands.

那覇　Naha

1917-03-12

Naha, the chief port of Okinawa Island.

沖縄の主港　那覇港

汽船が碇泊する那覇港を背景にした垣花の町並み。

Old townscape of Kakinohana. In the background, a steamship is anchored at Naha Port.

2017-01-08

港を見下ろす垣花町の丘の上から撮影。ウィルソンの写真には左奥に三重城、その対岸に県立水産学校の校舎、右側奥に監獄署（刑務所）の煙突が見える。瓦屋根と茅葺屋根が混在していた。

ヨーロッパを舞台とした戦争の痛みを抱えたウィルソンの心を癒した美しい垣花の古い町並みは、そのわずか28年後に爆撃で破壊され、今は人の住むことがない「那覇軍港（那覇港湾施設）」に姿を変えている。

From the hilltop of Kakinohana looking down at the port. Miegusuku, old fortress of the kingdom on the left, the prefectural fisheries school on opposite shore and the jail on right side. Roofs were a mixture of tile and thatch.

The peaceful old town, which soothed Wilson's worries about the war in Europe, was destroyed by bombs 28 years later. Now it is the U.S. Naval Port where nobody lives.

那覇　Naha

1917-02-26

Ficus retusa var. nitida Miq. From 35-40 ft. tall, girth of trunk from 6-8 ft.

ガジュマル　樹高 10.7-12.2m
幹周 1.8-2.4m

国場川に架かる真玉橋。当時、漫湖は現在のような干潟ではなく、湖のように水を湛えて広がっていた。干潟になったのは、1960年代の埋め立てからである。

Madan Bridge across the Kokuba River that flows into Manko. At that time Manko was still a large body of water. After landfills in the 1960's it became the narrow mangrove swamp seen today.

2017-06-28

　真玉橋の南側から撮影されたもの。かつては行商人が行き交う商いの交通路だった。豊見城市史によると、石橋の南側たもとは「アチョールマチグヮー（仲買人の市場）」と言われた場所で、辺りにマツやガジュマルが茂り、那覇の市場との間を往来する行商人がその木陰で涼をとったという。

　橋は沖縄戦で破壊され、戦後に改修された。戦前の石橋の部分遺構が、現在の橋の南北たもとに復元保存されている。

　Photographed from the south end, Madan Bridge was a busy merchant road. Historically, the south foot of this stone bridge used to be called "market of stall-keepers." Covered with thick Pine and Banyan trees, itinerant traders took a break and kept cool coming and going to the Naha market.

　This bridge was destroyed by bombs in wartime and rebuilt after the war. Remains of the stone bridge are reconstructed and preserved beside the new bridge.

那覇　Naha

1917-02-26

Pinus luchuensis Mayr. From 25-30 ft. tall, girth of trunk from 1-1.5 ft., showing smooth and scaly bark.

リュウキュウマツ　樹高　7.6-9.1m 幹周 0.3-0.45m 滑らかなウロコ状の樹皮

豊見城村の海岸部の丘陵から。埋め立て前は国場川に接していた。写真に写っている着物姿の人物は、ウィルソンの植物採集の手伝いをした少年だろうか。

From the hill of Tomigusuku Village along the Kokuba River.
The boy wearing kimono may be Wilson's helper for collecting plants.

2017-06-28

　真玉橋の南、国場川に沿った西側。昔は西原（ニシバル）と呼ばれていた地域の丘陵から奥武山を望む風景。かつては周りにサトウキビ畑が広がっていた。国場川と饒波川の水流が漫湖に注ぐ合流地点で、サーターヤー（製糖場）もあった。
　現在は埋め立てが進み内陸になってしまったが、漫湖を隔てて奥武山を望む風景は変わらない。

　This view from a hilltop in Nishibaru, south of Madan Bridge and west of Kokuba River overlooks Onoyama in the distance. Sugarcane fields spread out below. There were several Sugar mills around. This is the point where Kokuba and Noha Rivers converge, discharging into Manko.
　Onoyama can still be seen from this site, but the sugarcane fields have been filled and covered with houses.

那覇　Naha

1917-03-12

View of port from Onoyama. *Pinus luchuensis* Mayr. in foreground.

奥武山から望む那覇港の風景　前方にリュウキュウマツ

前方は南明治橋。写真の中央、橋のたもとに見えるのは御物城跡(おものぐすく)にできた高級料亭「風月楼」。

View of South-Meiji Bridge. Fugetsuro, a high-class restaurant (former Omonogusuku) can be seen at center.

2017-02-24

　左はウィルソンが沖縄を去る前日に、旅の締めくくりとして撮った最後の1枚。明治橋は旧御物城を挟んで南北に2本あった。かつては中国や東南アジアとの交易品を保管する琉球王朝の宝物庫であった御物城は、明治時代に大和風の高級料亭「風月楼」となり、寄留商人、県庁要人や本土からの賓客などが夜な夜な宴会を開いていた。

　辺りは沖縄戦で焼失、御物城であった頃の佇まいを残す城壁やアーチ型の石門の一部は残っているが、米軍基地の敷地内となっているため現在は立ち入ることはできない。

　Left is the last photo Wilson took the day before he left Okinawa. There were two Meiji Bridges, south and north. Omonogusuku was the treasure house in kingdom times, storing the trading goods from China and Southeast Asian countries. In the Meiji era, it became the Yamato style restaurant, "Fugetsuro," where Japanese mainland merchants and high-class bureaucrats held banquets every day.

　After the bombing, everything burned. Part of the old stone wall and stone gate of the treasure house remain, but cannot be visited now because the area is inside the U.S. base.

那覇　Naha

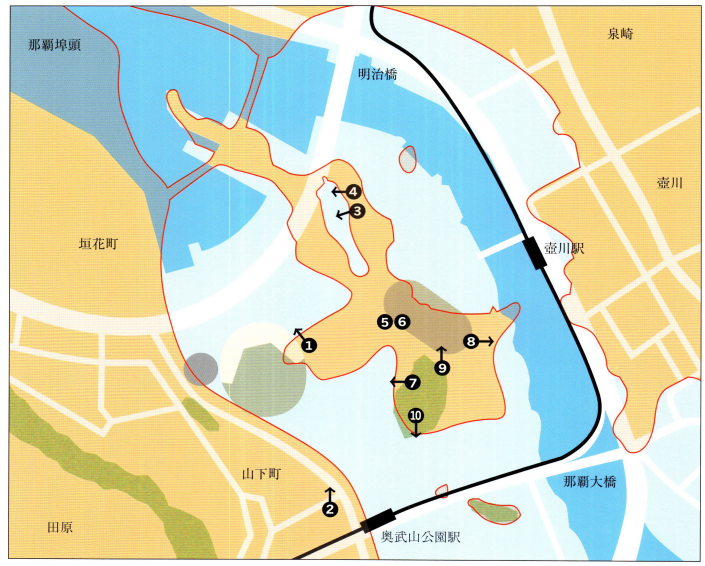

奥武山今昔地図　Old and New Map of Onoyama.

① P14　② P19　③ P24　④ P25　⑤ P26
⑥ P27　⑦ P30　⑧ P33　⑨ P34　⑩ P36

ウィルソンの撮影位置
Wilson's Camera Position.

1917-02-26

豊見城村の海岸部。急峻な場所に生えるソテツは土留めとしても役立った。

Near the coast of Tomigusuku Village. Cycus growing on steep slope is useful as earth retainer.

Cycas revoluta Thunb. Young trees of *Pinus luchuensis* Mayr. in rear. On hill side.

ソテツ 後ろにリュウキュウマツの若木が生育する丘の斜面

那覇 Naha

1917-02-26

Agave fourcroydes Lem. Naturalized near the sea.

リュウゼツラン科エネケン　海岸に帰化したもの

豊見城村の海岸部。背後は国場川の河口。沖縄ではアオノリュウゼツランとも呼ばれる中南米原産の植物。写真の男性は、東京から同行した通訳。

At the coast of Tomigusuku Village on the Kokuba River. This Agave, called Aonoagave in Okinawa, originally came from Latin America. The man in this photo is Wilson's translator from Tokyo.

1917-02-26

小禄村の海岸部。現在のモノレール奥武山公園駅から奥武山公園の方向を望む風景。1917年当時は、間に海があった。

At the coast of Oroku Village. View from the position of the current monorail station at Onoyama Park, which used to be separated by water.

Cycas revoluta Thunb. Spontaneous on coral rocks. Wood of *Pinus luchuensis* Mayr. beyond.

ソテツ　サンゴ礁に自生　遠方にリュウキュウマツの林

那覇　Naha

> *Pinus luchuensis* Mayr. 30ft. tall, girth of trunk 2ft., showing smooth and scaly bark.
>
> リュウキュウマツ
> 樹高9.1m 幹周0.6m　なめらかなウロコ状の樹皮

小禄村から豊見城村にかけての海岸部。

At the coast between Oroku Village and Tomigusuku Village.

1917-02-26

1917-03-11

小禄村から豊見城村にかけての海岸部。モンパノキは海岸の砂丘や隆起石灰岩上に育つ。地元の男性と思われる着物姿の人物が写っている。

At the coast between Oroku Village and Tomigusuku Village. Often grows on the coastal sand and coral stone. The man wearing kimono must be a local man.

Tournefortia argentea L. Height 5-6 ft. *Scaevola koenigii* Vahl. in rear.

モンパノキ　樹高　1.5-1.8m　後ろにクサトベラ

Scene 2 奥武山 Onoyama

マツは琉球の誉れであり、印象的で美しく、黒々とした物憂げな姿を見せている。
"This pine is the glory of Liukiu and both impressive and beautiful. Its aspect is dark and somber."
E.H.Wilson

漫湖の景勝地の今昔
Old and New of Manko's Scenic Island

　100年前の奥武山は港の入り江深く、漫湖に浮かぶ細長い小島だった。琉球王朝の時代から風光明媚な景勝地として親しまれ、江戸時代の有名な浮世絵師、葛飾北斎によって琉球八景のひとつとしても描かれている。
　2月25日、那覇港に上陸するとすぐに、沖縄の旅の第一歩としてウィルソンは奥武山をくまなく散策し、12枚の写真におさめた。一帯はリュウキュウマツの林に覆われ、さまざまな亜熱帯植物が鬱蒼と生い茂っていたという。御嶽、拝所、寺院、神殿なども各所に散らばり、古くからの神地としての顔も残されていた。

　100 years ago, Onoyama was a small pencil of an island floating in Manko, set far back from the inlet of the harbor. From the time of the Ryukyu Kingdom, it was cherished for its picturesque landscape and was even portrayed by the famous Edo-period ukiyo-e artist, Hokusai Katsushika, as one of his "Eight Views of Ryukyu."
　On February 25, as the first step in his travels in Okinawa, Wilson explored the nooks and crannies of Onoyama, capturing his time in twelve photographs. It was a region covered by forests of Ryukyu Pine, and various subtropical plants growing dense and luxuriantly.
　At the time, Meiji Bridge spanned North-to-South like

当時は御物城跡の高級料亭「風月楼」を頂点に、鳥が翼を広げたように南北明治橋でそれぞれ垣花と渡地につながっていた。島の中心に向かう小道は海岸線に沿って延び、やがてマングローブが植栽された池が見えてくる。池の下端の角に弁財天があった。龍洞寺を過ぎてさらに進むと小高い丘に行きあたる。そして、そこから入り江越しに真和志村を望む記念運動場が広がっていた。

　1901（明治34）年に奥武山は市民公園となり、各種競技大会や祭りなどの行事が開催され市民に親しまれる場所となった。同時に日露戦役記念碑、忠魂碑、そしてまた土地整理事業を記念して建てられた改租記念碑や事業を積極的に推し進めた奈良原繁第4代沖縄県知事の銅像などが立て続けに園内に設置された。明治末期から大正初期にかけて、次第に大和世（ヤマトユー）に呑み込まれていく時期の沖縄を如実に物語る場所でもあった。

　大正末期から徐々に埋め立てが進められていたが、戦後米軍の強力な重機によって一気に大規模な造成が実施され、垣花と陸続きになるなど大きな変貌を余儀なくされた。現在は周辺がさらに拡充され、陸上競技場、武道館、水泳プール、テニスコート、野球場などの各種施設が集約された市民の総合運動公園として整備されている。

　人影を避け、スポーツ施設の陰に残された空き地や裏の小道を歩いてみると、ウィルソンが切り取った大正期の風景の面影をかろうじて宿す場所に出会うことができた。

　奥武山の長い歴史の痕跡は、今も確かに息づいている。

a bird spreading its wings to connect Watanji and Kakinohana, with the apex at the high-class restaurant called "Fugetsuro" on the site of the remains of the Omonogusuku, old kingdom's treasure house. A small road leading to the heart of the island extended along the coastline, with planted mangroves eventually giving way to a pond. At the lower edge of the pond, the road made a turn, with Benzaiten Shrine at the corner. Continuing on past Ryutoji Temple, one arrived at a slightly elevated place of veneration. From there, the commemorative athletics field spread out overlooking Mawashi Village across the water.

　Since becoming a public park in 1901, a commemorative plaque of the Russo-Japanese War, a monument to the Taxation Reform, and a statue had been erected. It was a park loved by the citizens, where all sorts of sports tournaments, festivals, and other functions were held, but it was also a place that attested to the period when Okinawa was being swallowed up by "Yamato" Japan.

　Land reclamation efforts had been steadily advancing since the beginning of the 20th century, but after World War II, the heavy machinery of the American troops actualized large-scale reclamation, joining the island to the mainland at Kakinohana and bringing about other drastic changes. Now, the grounds have been further expanded to create a comprehensive public sports park, integrating such facilities as track-and-field grounds, a martial arts complex, swimming pool, tennis courts, and a baseball field.

　Leaving the throngs of people, I ventured down the small roads and patches of vacant land behind the sports complex, and I was thus able to encounter places where vestiges of the scenery captured by Wilson still managed to lurk. So I can say with certainty that, even now, traces of the long history of Onoyama continue to live on.

奥武山　Onoyama

1917-02-25

Rhizophora mucronata Lam. Height from 5-6 ft., planted.

ヤエヤマヒルギ（オオバヒルギ）
樹高 1.5-1.8m 植栽

奥武山の低地にかつて広がっていた池。植栽されていたマングローブの支柱根が水を通して写っている。

The pond used to exist at the lowland in Onoyama. Habitat of planted mangrove in water with visible roots.

1917-02-25

左の写真と続きの連写写真。背景に電線が走っている。1910(明治43)年に火力発電所が稼働し、この頃すでに那覇区には電灯が灯っていた。

Same area as preceding photo. Electric lines run in the background. At that time, electricity was already on in the Naha area.

Bruguiera gymnorhiza Lam. Girth 7 ft. *Rhizophora mucronata* Lam. in the rear. Planted.

オヒルギ　周囲　2.1m　後ろにヤエヤマヒルギ（オオバヒルギ）　植栽

奥武山　Onoyama

Garcinia spicata Hook.
25 ft. tall, girth of trunk 2 ft. Near a shrine.

フクギ　樹高 7.6m 幹周 0.6m 左に祠

公園内の道が曲がる角で撮影されたものと見られる。拝所（ウガンジュ）のような構造物が左に見える。

This photo was taken at a curve in the park road. The worship shrine on left.

1917-02-25

Ehretia acuminata R. Br. 25 ft. tall, girth of trunk 2 ft., roadside.

チシャノキ　樹高7.6m. 幹周0.6m 道路脇

1917-02-25

左の写真と同じ場所でアングルを変えて撮られたもの。同じ拝所（ウガンジュ）が左手奥に見える。

Photo taken from a different angle as the preceding shot. The same worship shrine is standing at back left.

奥武山　Onoyama

1917-02-25

Pinus luchuensis Mayr. From 60-70 ft. tall, girth of trunk from 4-5 ft.

リュウキュウマツ　樹高 18.3-21.3m
幹周 1.2-1.5m

当時の運動公園あたりから撮影したものと見られる。

Probably taken from the area of the old athletic park.

1917-02-25

Pinus luchuensis Mayr.
From 60-70 ft. tall, girth of trunk from 4-6 ft.

リュウキュウマツ
樹高 18.3-21.3m
幹周 1.2-1.8m

当時は手入れが行き届いた美しいマツで覆われていた。写真中ほどに小さく見える人物との対比から、マツの大きさがわかる。

Onoyama was covered with well cared for beautiful Pines in those days. You can see how big they are in comparison with the person's figure.

奥武山　Onoyama

1917-02-25

奥武山公園内の丘の上から松林越しに対岸の垣花を望む。現在は埋め立てられ陸続きになっている。木の間に座っているのは、鹿児島で合流した鹿児島大林区署林業技手の牛尾朋次。

Looking through Pines at the hill of Onoyama toward Kakinohana across water. Now they are joined together with landfill. The man sitting among trees is Hoji Ushio, forestry engineer in the Kagoshima Forestry Office who joined Wilson's Okinawa expedition.

Pinus luchuensis Mayr. From 30-60 ft. tall, girth of trunk from 3-7 ft. Forming pure woods.

リュウキュウマツ　樹高 9.1-18.3m
幹周 0.9-2.1m　純林を形成

1917-02-25

Pinus luchuensis Mayr.
From 60-70 ft. tall, girth of trunk from 4-6 ft.

リュウキュウマツ
樹高 18.3-21.3m
幹周 1.2-1.8m

樹齢40〜50年と思われるマツが土壌の薄い所に育っている。

Pines, extimated age of 40~50, grew on the thin surface soil.

奥武山　Onoyama

Pinus luchuensis Mayr. Girth of trunk 7 ft., bark gray. *Maba buxifolia* Pers. in rear.

リュウキュウマツ　幹周2.1m　樹皮は灰色　後ろにヤエヤマコクタン

ヤエヤマコクタンはしばしば楽器のサンシン（三線）の棹に利用される。環境省ＲＬ：準絶滅危惧（ＮＴ）。

This Ebony, behind, is often used for the neck of a Sanshin, Okinawan musical instrument. Ministry of Environment RL: Near threatened(NT).

1917-02-25

Pinus luchuensis Mayr. 70 ft. tall, girth of trunk 6 ft.

リュウキュウマツ 樹高 21.3m 幹周 1.8m

1917-02-25

運動場を見下ろす丘の上にあった忠魂碑。1915（大正4）年に帝国在郷軍人会那覇区分会などによって建てられたとされる。現存しない。

The monument for loyal souls which looked down on the athletic park. Built in 1915 by the Imperial Reservists' association, Naha branch, no longer exists.

奥武山　Onoyama

1917-02-25

Pinus luchuensis Mayr. From 30-50 ft. tall, girth of trunk from 3-5 ft. Man by trees with obelisk on pedestal on hill to left.

リュウキュウマツ　樹高 9.1-15.2m 幹周 0.9-1.5m　左の丘の上に台座付きのオベリスク

松林の中に立つ日露戦争記念碑。

Monument of Russo-Japanese War in Pine forests.

2017-01-08

　日露戦争記念碑が立っていたのは、現在の屋内プールの西側裏にあたる場所で、今は台座だけになり、拝所になっている。近くには1908（明治41）年に建てられた改租記念碑と奈良原繁元沖縄県知事の銅像が乗せられていた台座だけが残っていた。いずれも公園内の整備に伴って、元あった場所から移設して現在の場所にまとめて置かれたとみられる。公園内の近代的な各種スポーツ施設の賑わいとは対照的に訪れる人影もなく、うらびれた一画である。

　Monument of the Russo-Japanese War standing on top of a hill on Onoyama. Now only the pedestal remains as a place of worship. Nearby stand a monument of the Taxation Reform and the pedestal of a statue of Shigeru Narahara, the former Okinawa Governor who pushed that project earnestly, built in 1908. Both were relocated here when the park was developed.

　Now surrounded by busy athletic field and swimming pool, the site has become rather desolate.

奥武山　Onoyama

1917-02-25

Pinus luchuensis Mayr. Undergrowth of miscellaneous sub-tropical plants.

リュウキュウマツ　林床にさまざまな亜熱帯植物が生育している

奥武山から小禄村（現鏡原町）方面を望む。真ん中を走っている黒い線は、輸送中にガラス乾板に入ったひび。

View from Onoyama toward to Oroku Village, present Kyouhara Town. The black line in the photo is a crack in the glass plate negative.

2017·06·28

　ウィルソンの写真で対岸近くにアーチ型橋のように見えるのは、海岸に沿った道と並行に走っていた水路である可能性が高い。アーチ型の入り口に向かう小船の姿が2隻見える。

　現在は埋め立てによって陸続きとなったため、様相が大きく変わっている。かつての対岸の海岸線は現在の県道221号にあたると思われる。上を走るモノレールの姿も見える。

　The small arched opening on the far bank may be an entrance to the channel that ran parallel to the coast road in Wilson's photo. There were two boats cruising into the channel.

　At present, because of landfill, the landscape has changed dramatically. The old coastline became prefectural Route 221 and we can see the monorail running over the road.

Scene 3　宜野湾・嘉手納・読谷
Ginowan ／ Kadena ／ Yomitan

古都首里から延びる道には、美しいマツ並木の街道があった。
"On the highways leading from the old capital of Shuri, some fine avenues of Pine may be seen."
E.H.Wilson

基地に消えた聖なる道
The Vanished Sacred Road

　ウィルソンの沖縄の写真のなかで、ひときわ心を奪われる１枚があった。天を突き刺す勢いで聳えるリュウキュウマツの列なりが縦長のガラス乾板いっぱいに広がり、その下に一本の白い道が延びている。中ほどにぽつんと配置された客馬車が醸し出す静と動のコントラストが絶妙である。

　この美しい並木道の今はどうなっているのだろうか。「那覇と北谷をつなぐ道」というウィルソンの撮影メモだけを手掛かりに宜野湾市を訪れた。そして、私がそこで出会った事実は言葉を失うほど衝撃的なものであった。

　In the photographs of Okinawa Wilson took, there was one especially intriguing shot. A row of towering Ryukyu Pines piercing the sky spread out across the vertically-oriented glass plate, and beneath them extends a white road. Midway down the road, a single horse-drawn carriage creates an exquisite contrast between stillness and motion.

　What has become of this beautiful, tree-lined road? The note Wilson left with the photograph, "Avenue between Naha and Shatan," served as a clue as I set out to visit Ginowan City and I discovered the shocking truth.

　In the time of the Ryukyu Kingdom, this public road was a tree-lined route called "Sukumichi" that extended from Shuri, the capital of the kingdom, to each ward. It was used

その並木道は琉球王国の時代、首里から各間切（現在の市町村）に延びる宿道（すくみち）と呼ばれる公道のひとつだった。この道筋を使って、王府の文書が伝達され、また各地から年貢が運ばれた。17世紀後半には、尚貞王の王子尚純によって沿道にマツが植えられ、道の先には普天満宮という中頭地区最大の聖地があった。路面は石灰岩と香木の粉を混ぜた石粉で舗装され、旧暦の9月に首里を出発した琉球王がたくさんの供を従えて練り歩く御参詣（ぐさんちー）の道となり、やがて一般の人も重箱に詰めたご馳走を携えて、この道をたどって参拝するようになった。

　1881(明治14)年、神宮寺内に小学校が設立されると通学路として利用され、緑のトンネルが強い陽ざしから子供たちを守る役目を果たしてくれた。道の両側にはサトウキビ、田芋などの畑が広がり、作業の合間に木陰に身を休める農夫の頭上を涼風が葉ずれの音と共に吹き抜けていった。街道のマツはまさに周辺に住む人々の暮らしの一部であり、誇りだった。

　1932(昭和7)年、この道は国の天然記念物に指定された。記録では5.8kmの行程に約3000本のマツが立ち、幹周2.4m以上の巨木は123株を数えたとある。

　そして、1945年の沖縄戦。樹齢300年を誇るマツの並木は、日本軍や米軍の手でその大半が切り倒され、また砲撃で焼かれ、戦車で踏みにじられた。戦後、周辺の人家や畑と共に強制的に接収されるとその原型は消滅していった。

　この道のかつての呼称は、「宜野湾並松（じのーんなんまち）」。現在の場所は、米海兵隊の普天間飛行場内。戦前の航空写真と現在の俯瞰写真とを重ねてみると、街道跡は飛行場の真ん中をまっすぐ貫く滑走路とその横に並列する駐機場の一線にぴたりと重なった。

to transmit documents from the royal government and to carry the annual tributes. The road led to the Futenma Shrine, the largest holy area in the central part of Okinawa's main island. During the second half of the 17th century, Pine trees were planted along the route and the road was paved with white coral dust. It was the road on which the Ryukyu monarch and his many attendants would parade as they departed from Shuri on the annual pilgrimage to Futenma Shrine. Before long it would also be traveled by commoners on their way to pay homage.

In 1881, an elementary school was opened within the Buddhist temple attached to the shrine, and this road became the route to get to school, sheltering school children from the blazing sun in a tunnel of green. Fields of sugarcane and taro fanned out on both sides of the road, and between work shifts, a cool breeze would rustle the leaves as it blew over the heads of farmhands resting in the shade of the trees.

In 1932, the road was designated a national natural monument. According to records, along its course of 5.8 kilometers stood approximately 3,000 Pine trees including 123 giants with trunks measuring at least 2.4 meters in circumference.

Then came the Battle of Okinawa in 1945. The majority of that stately row of 300-year-old trees were cut down, burned from bombardment, or trampled by tanks. After the war, the road was confiscated along with the surrounding houses and fields, and its original essence was extinguished.

This road was once known as "Jinon-nanmachi", Ginowan Pine Lane. The location is now part of the U.S. Marine Corps' Futenma Air Base. If one overlays aerial photographs from before the war with current photographs, the former main road lies precisely on the line of the runway that cuts straight through the center of the airfield.

宜野湾・嘉手納・読谷　Ginowan／Kadena／Yomitan

Pinus luchuensis Mayr. Avenue between Shatan and Naha. Fields of sugarcane in distance.

リュウキュウマツ 那覇と北谷をつなぐ街道 遠くにサトウキビ畑

写真の真ん中にウィルソンが移動に使ったと思われる客馬車。当時の客馬車はトタン屋根で後部から乗り降りした。

At the center of photo there is a carriage which Wilson used. The roof was galvanized iron and passengers got in and out from the back side.

1917-02-27

2010年撮影

　ウィルソンが何度か客馬車から降りて、沿道の松並木を撮影した宜野湾街道は、普天満宮への参詣道であるだけでなく、近隣の人々の暮らしに密接に関わっていた道でもあった。村人は台風の強風で傷んだ枝を切り落とし、常に通りを掃き清めることを忘れなかった。落ち葉も無駄にせず、かまどの火にくべる燃料として利用した。

　人々の思いがこもったこの聖なる道は手の届かない存在になったばかりか、本来の目的とはまったく異なる用途に供されるようになり、今はただ人々の遠い記憶のなかにのみ留まっている。

　On the Ginowan Highway Wilson stopped his carriage and took several photos. This road was not only the pilgrimage route to Futenma Shrine, but was also important to the neighborhood people's everyday life. Villagers removed damaged branches after typhoons and used fallen pine-needles as fuel for their cooking stoves.

　This sacred route, once the area of people's spirits, is now gone and used for completely different purposes. Today, only it's memory exits.

宜野湾・嘉手納・読谷　Ginowan／Kadena／Yomitan

Pinus luchuensis Mayr. Avenue of, between Naha and Shatan.

リュウキュウマツ　那覇と北谷をつなぐ街道

宜野湾街道は1902（明治35）年に人力車や客馬車が通れるように整備されたという。道の両側に排水溝が走り、外の土手にマツが一列に並んでいた。

Ginowan Highway was widened to accommodate carriages and rickshaws in 1917. Rain gutters were dug at both sides of the road and Pines stood along the both banks.

1917-02-27

Pinus luchuensis Mayr. Girth of trunk 7 ft., showing deeply fissured bark. Shatan.

リュウキュウマツ　幹周 2.1m 深い亀裂の入った樹皮　北谷

ウィルソンが「アジアで最も美しいマツで、際立った姿で簡単に見分けられる」と絶賛したリュウキュウマツ。

Wilson said, "It is one of the most beautiful of Asiatic Pines and is very distinct and easily recognized species".

1917-02-27

宜野湾・嘉手納・読谷　Ginowan／Kadena／Yomitan

1917·02·27

Pinus luchuensis Mayr. Flat top specimen 25 ft. tall, 60 ft. spread. Girth of trunk 10 ft. Ginowan-mura.

リュウキュウマツ　平らな頭をした個体
樹高 7.6m 樹冠 18.3m 幹周 3m

強い風のせいで樹冠が平らになった平松。前に延びる道は現国道58号。宜野湾の大山集落にあったので、「大山平松（おおやまひらまーちゅー）」と呼ばれていた。道脇に立つ男性は、地元の石大工だった名城加目。

Because of strong winds, the crown was flattened on top. The road in front is present Rout 58. People called it "Oyama Flat Pine" because it stood in Oyama. The man staning on the roadside is Kame Nashiro, local mason.

1917-02-27

Pinus luchuensis Mayr. 90 ft. tall, girth of trunk 10 ft. Shatan.

リュウキュウマツ　樹高 27.4m. 幹周 3m.

街道の北谷寄りで見かけたひときわ目を引いたマツの大木。中頭地区でウィルソンが出会った最大のマツだった。

The biggest, most handsome Pine Wilson met in Nakagami Area, Central Okinawa. It was one of the most striking Pines on the highway in Chatan.

宜野湾・嘉手納・読谷　Ginowan/Kadena/Yomitan

1917-03-08

Katena Village (actually Hijyabashi, Yuntanza Village). Wood of *Pinus luchuensis* Mayr. beyond.

嘉手納の集落（筆者注＝正しくは読谷山村の比謝矼集落）。背後にリュウキュウマツの林

名護の帰りに立ち寄った比謝港。右端に見えるのが石造りの比謝橋。物資の集積港として賑わっていた。

Wilson stopped by Hijya Port on the way back from Nago. The stone Hijya Bridge is on the right. The port was a thriving goods distribution center.

ウィルソンは撮影した集落を嘉手納だと思い、また耳にした音声から"Katena"と記載したと考えられる。

2017-07-05

　嘉手納町と読谷村の間に架かる比謝橋は、比謝川の河口部から蛇行する川筋を上ったところにある。那覇と名護を結ぶ宿道（現国道58号）の中継点でもあり、昔から海上と陸上の双方の交通運輸の要所であった。ウィルソンの写真中央に写る「木ノ下材木店」があった扇状地と背後の家々は、元士族たちの手で作られた商工業に特化した自治区、比謝矼（ばし）で当時の繁栄は瓦屋根が並んでいる様子からもうかがえる。

　1867年再建の5連続アーチ式の美しい石橋は、現在は鉄筋コンクリート造りとなっている。材木店の跡には芭蕉が繁茂していた。

Hijya Bridge between Kadena and Yomitan is situated several miles above the river mouth. It was a transit point of the old Sukumichi, now Route 58, connecting Naha and Nago. Kinoshita Lumber Company in the center of Wilson's photo was situated on the alluvial fan and the houses behind was a borough developed by former samurai families . The number of tiled roofs shows its prosperity.

　The beautiful fived arched stone bridge last repaired in 1867 has been replaced with reinforced concrete. Japanese Fiber Banana now grows where the lumber company stood.

Scene 4　慶良間諸島　Kerama Islands

私はこの島を訪れる初めての西洋人であると言われ、素朴な好奇の目で迎えられた。
"I was the first foreigner to visit this island they said and so their curiosity was natural enough."
E.H.Wilson

ウランダーが見た風景
Through the Eye of a Foreigner

　3月2日、ウィルソンは那覇の西約30〜40kmに点在する慶良間諸島に向かう船上にあった。まだ定期船はなく、銅鉱山会社が手配した絶えず故障する発動機をつけた漁船を操っての旅だった。「雨が旅の楽しみを妨害したが、島々は険しく、複雑に入り組んでいて、非常に画趣に富んでいた」とメモに残している。

　旧暦2月のこの頃は「二月風廻り（ニンガチカジマーイ）」と呼ばれる季節で、空模様は不安定だったが、雲間から差し込む光の下に浮かぶ孤島や岩礁が織りなす風景は格別な輝きで、異国のプラント・ハンターの目を喜ばせた。

On March 2nd, Wilson was aboard a boat bound for the Kerama Islands, located 30 to 40 kilometers west of Naha. Travel was arranged by a copper-mining company via a fishing boat with an engine that was constantly breaking down. Wilson wrote in his notebook, "The rain interfered with the pleasure of the trip, but all the islands are bold, much indented, and very picturesque."

The weather is unstable in this season in Okinawa, a time when the skies are moody but the view of coral reefs interwoven among solitary islands resting below rays of sunlight is exceptional.

The inhabitants of the Kerama Islands, a stopping point for trade, are essentially people of the ocean. During the era

海洋貿易の中継地であった慶良間諸島の人々は元来、海の民である。琉球王国の時代は船乗りとして進貢船に乗り込んだり、遠洋を舞台に活躍した。ウィルソンが訪れた1917（大正６）年は、鰹漁業の最盛期で不況知らずとも言われた頃だった。貿易船から漁船に乗り換えた男たちは再び海に活路を見いだしていった。慶良間で製造された鰹節は、那覇を経由して各地に送られて砂糖に次ぐ沖縄の移出品にまで成長した。また、久場島、屋嘉比島の鉱山では折からの第一次大戦による需要を受け銅が盛んに採掘されていた。

　ウィルソンは、久場島を経て渡嘉敷島の阿波連に立ち寄り、そこで植物採集と写真撮影を済ませると、阿嘉島に渡り民家で一晩を過ごした。撮影機材を抱え植物を採集する西洋人の姿を目にして、村人の好奇心は高まった。夜がふける頃になると、区長と小学校の訓導を先頭に手に手に泡盛の甕を携えた人々がやってきた。

　「私たちは住民の注目を浴び、愛想よく迎えられた。葉巻とウィスキーを差し出したら、米で作った琉球ワインをふるまってくれた」

　日本各地をくまなく旅したウィルソンだが、このように地元の人々と過ごしたひとときについて語っているのはここ阿嘉島だけある。他の場所では味わうことのなかった愉快な夜を過ごしたものと想像する。

　最初の米軍上陸地となった慶良間諸島も沖縄戦で多数の住民を巻き込む凄惨な犠牲を生み、同時に貴重な記録も失われたが、「100年ほど前にウランダーが来た」という伝承が残っていた。ウランダーというのはオランダ人という意味だが、かつて沖縄では西洋人をそう一括りにして呼んでいた。ウィルソンの足跡は、豊かな自然と人々の笑顔のなかに存在していた。

of the Ryukyu Kingdom, they were seamen who worked the high seas, embarking on official ships to China. Wilson's visit in 1917 corresponded to golden years for the bonito fishing industry. The men who left trading vessels to board fishing boats once again found the sea their means of survival. The dried bonito produced in Kerama and sent via Naha to ports throughout Japan grew to be a major export commodity, second only to brown sugar in Okinawa. The Island's copper mines prospered do to the demands of World War I.

Wilson traveled by way of Kuba Island to Aharen on Tokashiki Island, and when he finished collecting plants and photographing there, he crossed to Aka Island and spent a night at a private residence. As the night advanced, people arrived led by the village headman and the schoolmaster, each one carrying an earthen pot of Okinawan liquor, Awamori.

"We attracted much attention but good humor prevailed. I treated them to cigars and whiskey and they responded by giving Liukiu wine, made from rice." Wilson wrote.

Even though he had traveled to all corners of Japan, Aka Island is the only place in which Wilson speaks of spending such a good time with the locals.

Alas, inhabitants of the Kerama Islands were drawn into the ghastly sacrifices of the Battle of Okinawa, and many records have been lost, but there remains a tale that states, "About one hundred years ago, the Ulander arrived." Although Ulander literally means Dutchman, there was a time in Okinawa when it was used as a term for all Westerners. Indeed, the footprints of Wilson are to be found in both abundant nature and in the smiling faces of people.

慶良間諸島　Kerama Islands

1917-03-03

Sideroxylon ferrugineum Hook & Arn. 35 ft. tall, girth of trunk 7 ft., possibly planted. Aka island.

アカテツ　樹高 10.7m　幹周 2.1m　植栽の可能性あり　男の右に干し草の山　阿嘉島

この時、すでに樹齢300年以上だったと思われる「御殿（うどぅん）の木」。干し草の山に見えたのは、「種取（たんとぅい）行事」のための御殿だった。右端の白い瓦屋根の家は現存している。

"Udun Tree," which was over 300 years old at that time. What looked like a haystack was "udun," a sacred place, where villagers prepared a special festival. House with white tiled roof still exists.

2017-03-07

　戦火を奇跡的に生き抜いて、今も同じ場所に立っている「御殿の木」。現在の樹高は約12m、幹周は５m。樹高にあまり変化は見られないが、幹は3mほど太くなり、枝も添え木が必要なほど逞しくなっている。御殿があった場所は、現在は拝所になっている。県内最大のアカテツ。座間味村指定文化財。

"Udun tree" still stands, having miraculously survived the fires of wartime. Present height is about 12m and girth is about 5m. Height has not changed so much, but the trunk is much fatter and the bigger branches need support posts. The worship shrine was built at the place where "Udun" was located. This Northern Yellow Boxwood is the biggest in Okinawa. Designated a cultural property by Zamami Village.

慶良間諸島　Kerama Islands

1917-03-03

Pinus luchuensis Mayr. with undergrowth of Pandanus tectorius Soland. Aka island.

リュウキュウマツ　林床にアダン　阿嘉島

山腹から慶留間島を背景に海峡を望む。海岸沿いの茅葺屋根の家々は、本家の次男、三男が独立して作った分家村で東村（あがりむら）と呼ばれた。

View from hillside toward the Kerama Strait, Geruma Island is in the background. The thatched houses along the shore were the branch family's village, called "Agari Village."

Livistona chinensis R. Br. & *Pinus luchuensis* Mayr. with undergrowth of *Didymosperma engleri* Warb. & miscellaneous trees. Aharen island.

ビロウとリュウキュウマツ クロツグやさまざまな木が林床を埋めている 阿波連 (渡嘉敷島)

クバ山の西側海岸。写真の右下に拝所が見える。

West side shore of Kuba Mountain. There is a shrine at the right side of the photo.

1917-03-02

慶良間諸島　Kerama Islands

1917-03-02

Hernandia peltata with Livistona chinensis R. Br. Pinus luchuensis Mayr. beyond. Aharen island.

ハスノハギリとビロウ　遠くにリュウキュウマツ　阿波連(渡嘉敷島)

ウィルソンが「モップのような灰緑色の葉を冠のごとく掲げた木」と表現したビロウは、地元ではクバと呼ばれている。樹林下部の水辺に立つのは園原咲也。

Chinese Fan Palm. Wilson said "With its mop-like crown of gray-green leaves over-topping the other vegetation." Okinawa people named this Palm "Kuba." Sakuya Sonohara standing near water.

2017-03-08

同じ場所の現在のクバ山。渡嘉敷島阿波連自然植物園。モクマオウやオオハマボウが繁茂し、クバ（ビロウ）の姿は減少している。葉を何千枚も組み合わせて船の帆が作られたというクバは、御嶽、拝所など神聖な場所に植えられた。

Kuba, Chinese Fan Palm, growing in the same mountain as Wilson's photo. After the war Casuarina and Beach Hibiscus have increased and the number of Kuba is reducing. People used to make boat sails by weaving together several thousand leaves. Often planted at sacred places in Okinawa.

慶良間諸島　Kerama Islands

Didymosperma engleri Warb. with *Livistona chinensis* R. Br. Aharen island.

クロツグと ビロウ
阿波連(渡嘉敷島)

現在の阿波連青少年村キャンプ場近く。当時31歳の園原咲也がクロツグの下から顔をのぞかせている。

Near the current Aharen Camping Site for Youth. The man peering out under the Palms is Sakuya Sonohara.

1917-03-02

1917-03-02

オキナワハイネズは砂地に這って伸びる小型のヒノキ科の針葉樹。後にウィルソンは論文の中に記載し、自らの名前を入れた学名を付けた。沖縄県RDB:絶滅危惧IB類（EN）。

This small Conifer of the family Cupressaceae has branches that trail along the sandy soil. Wilson described this plant in his report and later named it after himself, *Juniperus conferta* Parl.var *maritima* E.H. Wilson. Okinawa Pref. RDB:Endangered species (EN).

Juniperus conferta Parl. *Pandanus tectorius* Soland. in rear. Aharen island.

オキナワハイネズ　後ろにアダン
阿波連(渡嘉敷島)

Scene 5 　首里・中城　Shuri ／ Nakagusuku

首里の古宮の庭には、驚くような古いアカギの大木が生息していた。
"In the old palace grounds at Shuri grow some magnificent old trees of the Bischofia."
E.H.Wilson

古都復興へのオマージュ
Homage to Ancient Capital

　ウィルソンは、沖縄本島北部への調査を挟んで前後２回、かつての琉球王国の都に足を延ばした。美しい古建築やツタに覆われた石橋や石塀の風情に450年の王国の詩情を感じながら、街を見下ろす丘の上の探索を楽しんだ。しかし、当然あるはずと予想していた首里城の写真はなかった。いわゆる名所旧跡を訪れても絵ハガキ的な構図は協力避けようとする傾向がウィルソンにはある。あえて、人気のない裏道に足を運んでは残したい風景を自らの眼で選んで撮影している。私は首里城に正面から挑まなかったのはこの一種の美学に基づくものであろうと考えていた。

　Wilson's travels took him to Shuri in the heart of the former Ryukyu Kingdom twice. Feeling the poetry of 450 years of monarchy dancing in the charm of ivy-covered stone walls and bridges and the beautiful old architecture, he enjoyed exploring the hilltop overlooking town. However, he left us no photographs of Shuri Castle. Wilson had a strong aversion to postcard-like compositions even when visiting famous historic sites. I suspect that he never tackled a frontal view of Shuri Castle can perhaps be attributed to this principle.

　Shuri Castle was surrendered to the Ministry of the Army when feudal domains were replaced with the prefectural system around 1879 and the castle started to fall into ruin.

廃藩置県とともに陸軍省に明け渡された首里城は、熊本鎮台分遣隊営所の管轄となった。明治末期に首里区に移管された後も荒れるにまかされ、取り壊しの検討もされるなか、ようやく再建の道が開かれたのは昭和になってからだった。大正期に撮られた崩壊寸前の城の写真を目にした時に、栄華を誇った王国の終焉の姿に触れたような気がした。積極的に反戦論を唱えていたウィルソンは、軍靴で踏みにじられた古城にレンズを向けるに忍びない思いがあったのだろうか。

沖縄戦の時には首里城は陸軍総司令部となり、そのため城周辺も含めて徹底的に破壊された。現在、我々が見ることができるのは戦後に再び復元された姿である。

戦争が終焉した時、爆風で身を焼かれながらも一面の焼野原の中で粛然と立っていたアカギの木が1本あった。いつしか枯れた幹にアコウが気根をからみつかせて着生し、今もその命を引き継いでいる。戦前まで、この一帯は安国山（通称ハンタン山）と呼ばれる鬱蒼としたアカギの大木の森があった。太平の世のシンボルとして15世紀に植林されたものである。ウィルソンはこの森の北西側、つまり円鑑池の方からアカギ群落を撮影していた。

首里城は現在、国内外から年間200万人近い観光客が訪れる沖縄を代表する観光地となっている。目にも艶やかに彩色された本殿や守礼門を背景に写真を撮る人々の姿は、絶えることはない。そのなかのどれほどの数の人が、城郭の外に佇む1本の木に足を止めるのだろうか。ウィルソンが残した写真が、復興への道を歩んできた古都首里に捧げられた静かなるオマージュであるかのように思えてならない。

When I happened upon a photograph around Wilson's time, showing the main hall on the brink of collapse, I could feel the demise of that proud and glorious kingdom. Perhaps Wilson could not bring himself to turn his camera lense towards the old castle that had been trampled by army boots.

During the Battle of Okinawa, Shuri Castle was headquarters for the Japanese military, and for this reason everything in the vicinity of the castle was destroyed. What we see there today is a reconstruction made long after the war.

At the conclusion of the war, in the middle of the expanse of burnt fields, there remained one lone Bishop Wood (Bischofia) still solemnly standing, its figure burnt from the blasts. At some point, a Strangler Fig twined its roots around that withered trunk and to this day continues to inherit the life of original tree. Until the days leading to war, this region was a forest called Hantanyama where large Bishop Woods grew densely. They were said to have been planted in the fifteenth century as a symbol of a peaceful era. Wilson photographed these trees from the northwest side of the forest, at the edge of Enkan Pond.

Today, Shuri Castle is a major tourist destination and symbol of Okinawa, visited yearly by nearly two million people from both Japan and abroad. There is a ceaseless crowd of people taking photographs with the enchanting colors of the main hall or gate in the background. How many of these people have paused by that single tree still standing outside the castle walls? I can't help thinking that the photograph left by Wilson pays a quiet homage to Shuri, the ancient capital that has followed a long path to restoration.

首里・中城　Shuri/Nakagusuku

Bischofia javanica Bl. 70 ft. tall, girth of trunk from 8-10 ft. Near the ex-King's palace.

アカギ　樹高 21m. 幹周 2.4-3m. 首里、旧王国の王宮近く 円鑑池

1502年に造られた人工池、円鑑池から撮ったと思われるハンタン山のアカギ林。

Bishop Wood grove on Hantan-yama, at Enkan Pond, an artificial pond built in 1502.

1917-03-04

2017·06·02

　琉球石灰岩の間から龍樋を通じて湧き出す清水が円鑑池に溜められ、あふれた水が隣の龍潭に流れる仕組みになっていた。ウィルソンの写真で水が張っていないように見えるのは、一面に藻が繁茂していたせいと思われる。

　アカギ群落は沖縄戦で焼失した。現在の円鑑池は1968年に修復されたもの。かつてのような大木で構成された森の姿は見られないが、２世のアカギが水面に緑の影を落としている。

Through the Ryuhi, the drainpipe of Shuri Castle, spring water from Ryukyu lime stone was collected in this pond and overflow water went to the next big manmade lake, Ryutan. The reason it looks like no water in Wilson's photo is algae spread over the water.

The present Pond was rebuilt in 1968 after wartime destruction. There is no thick forest anymore; second generation trees throw their green reflection over the water.

首里・中城　Shuri/Nakagusuku

> *Cyphokentia savoryana* Rehd. & Wils. 55 ft. tall, planted. *Bischofia javanica* Bl. in rear.
>
> ノヤシ（セボリーヤシ）
> 樹高 16.8m. 植栽　後ろにアカギ

王家の菩提寺だった円覚寺周辺。円覚寺は沖縄戦で焼失したが、1968年に総門などが復元された。ウィルソンが学名を付けたノヤシは現在、環境省RL：絶滅危惧Ⅱ類(VU)。小笠原固有種。

Around Enkaku-ji, the family temple of Ryukyu King. The main temple gate was rebuilt in1968 after wartime destruction. The Palm which Wilson named is a Vulnerable Species now. Ministry of Environment RL: Vulnerable species(VU) Endemic to Ogasawara Islands.

1917-03-04

1917-03-11

亀甲墓と破風墓が並ぶ。ウィルソンは「琉球では、住宅とは異なり墓は巨大だ。人々の富が惜しみなく注がれている」と感想を述べている。

Turtleback tomb and gable style tomb. Wilson said "Unlike the houses the graves are enormous. It would appear that all the wealth of the people is lavished on the building of tombs."

Liukiu mausoleum. Pure wood of *Pinus luchuensis* Mayr. behind.

琉球の墓　後ろにリュウキュウマツの純林

首里・中城　Shuri/Nakagusuku

Erythrina indica L. 50 ft. tall, girth of trunk 12 ft. *Rhus succedanea* L. in left foreground.

デイゴ　樹高15.2m 幹周3.7m 左前方にハゼノキ

首里の近辺の庭園で撮影されたものと思われるデイゴ。庭園も樹木も沖縄戦の激しい爆撃で姿を消した。沖縄の県花。

Photographed in a garden at Shuri. Both garden and trees disappeared in the heavy wartime bombing. *Erythria indica* is Okinawa's prefectural flower.

1917-03-04

1917-03-04

那覇から首里に向かう途中の浦添で撮影されたと思われる。後方の丘は沖縄戦における最大の激戦地のひとつになった前田高地（ハクソー・リッジ）か。
Urasoe area on the way from Naha to Shuri. The hill in the back is might be "Hacksaw Ridge," where one of the fiercest battles was fought during the war.

Ficus retusa var. *nitida* Miq. Tree 45 ft. tall, girth of trunk 8-10 ft. The Liukiu Banyan Tree.

ガジュマル　樹高 13.7m 幹周 2.4-3m
英語の一般名はリュウキュウバンヤン

首里・中城　Shuri/Nakagusuku

1917-03-11

Cycas revoluta Thunb. on wall of ruined castle built 400 years ago. *Pinus luchuensis* on left. Nakagusuku Casle.

ソテツ　400年前の城跡の壁。左にリュウキュウマツ　中城城跡

太平洋を望む断崖上に築かれた城（グスク）。15世紀前半に廓が拡張され中心部が完成した。

The center part of the Gusuku(castle)was built early in the 15th century on a cliff facing the Pacific Ocean.

12017-01-08

現在の中城城跡。城の正門であった南の廓から一の廓を捉えたもの。加工していない自然石を組み合わせた野面積みや加工した積み石を隙間なく積み上げる布積みの技法で造られた石垣がせり出しているのが特徴。国指定史跡。世界遺産。

Present Nakagusuku castle ruins. Photo from South Kuruwa which was the main gate to Ichi-no-Kuruwa. The old construction is of natural stones along with the striking technique of laying processed stones without a gap. National Historic Site and UNESCO World Heritage Site.

Scene 6　名護　Nago

軒の長い茅葺屋根の小さな平屋の家々は、フクギの木に抱かれていた。
"In Nago the small one storied houses with the relatively long thatched roofs are mostly hidden among Garcinia."
E.H.Wilson

和やかな風に抱かれた街
A Heartwarming Town

　名護の地名の由来は、「和む」からきているという。まさにその謂れの通り海、山、川に抱かれた空間に、フクギの木々に身を隠すようにひっそりと家屋が立ち並ぶ美しく穏やかな街だった。北部に広がる山岳部は通称山原（ヤンバル）と呼ばれる自然が豊かな一帯で、ウィルソンは「屋久島に似ている」と述べている。
　廃藩置県後に役所や学校が建てられると、名護は沖縄本島の北と南をつなぐ物資の集積地、交通の要所として発展し「国頭地方最も繁盛の地」と言われるようになった。原動力となったのは禄を失い首里や那覇から流れてきた寄留士族たちだった。

　The name of Nago is said to come from the word, nagomu, meaning, "heartwarming." Just as the name implies, Nago—with modest rows of houses surrounded by Garcinia in the space embraced by mountains, a river, and the sea—was a beautiful, quiet town.
　When schools and government offices were set up after prefectures were established to replace feudal domains in 1879, this holding area for goods linking Naha and Yanbaru, the mountainous region of northern Okinawa, developed as an important transportation point, and was even said to be, "the most prosperous place in the north." This prosperity was driven by the sojourns of samurai families who drifted in from Naha and Shuri after losing their sti-

その昔は山原船による海上交通に限られていたが、1896（明治29）年に那覇との間に定期航路が開設されると、港の通りに海運関係の会社や倉庫、旅館、料理屋、商店が立ち並ぶようになった。

　そして1915年（大正4）には現在の国道58号線の前身にあたる国頭街道が開通して那覇と名護を結ぶ陸上交通路が整備された。さらに山原に延びる郡道も整い始め、名護は名実ともに沖縄本島を縦断する物資の中継地として発展した。

　ウィルソンが訪れた時は、まさに海上から陸上へと輸送の主役が交代しかけようとする時期だった。しかし、馬車で陸路を走るのはまだ不便で、特に許田から先は、「名護の七曲り」と呼ばれたほど山裾に沿って道がくねくねと曲がり、道幅も狭く時間がかかった。そこで、ウィルソンは那覇港から小さな発動機船に乗って北を目指した。通常は4時間の行程だが、その日は海が荒れていたため5時間半もかかったという。

　たどり着いた三日月型に広がる名護湾の奥には、活気に満ちた集落と山原の森が旅人を待ち受けていた。港界隈では瀟洒な佇まいの旅館が立ち並び、豊富で清涼な水で満たされた風呂が波に揺られた体を癒してくれた。

　「ここの旅館はとても居心地がいい」と、ウィルソンも満足した様子である。

　宿の風情が良かったのか、もてなしが素晴らしかったのか。あるいは、この時期ならではの新鮮なクジラの肉に舌鼓を打ったのか。想像してみるのも楽しい。一歩集落の外に出ると田植え唄が風に伝って聞こえ、製糖場の煙突から立ち上る甘い香りを含んだ煙が一筋見えた。そんなのどかな農村風景に心を奪われたのかもしれない。

pends.

Transportation to Nago had been limited to small sailboats called "Yanbaru boat," but in 1896, a regular sea route to Naha was established and maritime companies, warehouses, restaurants, inns, and shops popped up along the harbor streets.

Then, in 1915, Kunigami Highway, the predecessor of today's National Route 58 opened, establishing a land route to Naha. Work also started on a district road stretching to Yanbaru, and Nago developed into the main stopover for goods crossing the main island of Okinawa from top to bottom.

When Wilson visited, it was at exactly the time when the principal means of transportation was changing from sea to land. However, wagons traveling the overland route were still inconvenient. So, Wilson boarded a small motor boat and headed north. The ocean was particularly rough that day, and the typically four-hour voyage took five and a half hours.

When the party finally arrived at crescent-shaped Nago Bay, the lively village and surrounding forests were waiting for them. In the neighborhood by the harbor inns lined the streets, and a bath full of plentiful, refreshing water soothed Wilson's wave-rocked body. "The Japanese Hotel there is very good," Wilson wrote in his book.

Perhaps he found the style of the inn to be pleasing, or perhaps he found the hospitality remarkable. Or perhaps, considering the timing of his visit, he relished the taste of fresh whale meat. It's fun to imagine. Taking a step outside of town, maybe he could hear rice-planting songs borne by the wind or see a wisp of smoke carrying a sweet fragrance as it rose from a sugar plant chimney. He must have been captivated by such tranquil rural scenery.

名護　Nago

1917-03-08

Sea beach, Nago. The canoe in foreground is a hollowed-out log of *Pinus luchuensis* Mayr.

名護湾。前方にリュウキュウマツで作った刳り舟

背景に嘉津宇岳と八重岳が見える。この時季、刳り舟を使ってクジラ漁が行われていた。

Katsuudake and Yaedake in the back. People used to fish whales in this bay using the canoe.

2017·01·07

ウィルソンの時代には、春先になると名護湾にヒートゥ（コビレゴンドウ）が回遊した。人々は、沖合から割り舟で湾内にクジラを追い込み、浜近くで銛を手に格闘しながら射止め貴重なタンパク源とした。多い時は1日200頭も捕獲したという。「会社通り」と呼ばれた浜の通りには、海運関係の会社や倉庫、旅館、商店が立ち並び賑わいを見せていた。

1972年、この辺りは道路建設やスポーツ公園整備のため埋め立てられ、海岸線が大きく変わった。ウィルソンの撮影地点は、現在の浜より内陸側に200mほど入った所と思われる。

In early spring whales (Short-finned Pilot Whale) migrated to Nago Bay in Wilson's time. People drove whales inside the bay with dugout canoes and harpooned them near the beach; as many as 200 on a good day. They were a primary source of protein. The beach side street was called "company road," because it held many shipping companies, warehouses, inns, and shops.

In 1972, this coast was landfilled for road construction and setting up the sport park. Wilson's camera position was about 200m inland from today's coastline.

名護　Nago

1917-03-06

Terminalia catappa L. 50 ft. tall, spread 60 ft., girth of trunk 10 ft. Inamine Village.

コバテイシ（モモタマナ）樹高15.2m
樹冠18.3m　幹周3m　稲嶺村

旧羽地村随一の名木として知られ、琉歌にも詠まれた村のシンボル的な木。木の左下に立つのは植物採集箱を肩にした園原咲也。

This magnificent tree in the village was well known, appearing in Ryukyu poetry, and of great historical interest in the old Haneji area. The man standing to the left of the tree is Sakuya Sonohara holding the plant collection box.

2017-03-10

　名護からちょうど２里の地点にあたる海浜にあるため、昔の里程の基準にもされていたコバテイシの木は大小２本あった。木の下は広場となっていて、子供たちの遊び場や青年の角力場として、また村人が涼をとる場所としていつも人で賑わっていたという。年中行事も繰り広げられ、村人が集まっては三線（サンシン）が奏でられ踊りが披露される場所だった。

　戦後、台風の被害を受け倒壊。区有地であった広場も戦後の財政立て直しのために農協や駐在所に貸され、姿を消した。1970年代後半頃に植えられた２代目の木が現在、立っている。

　This tree stood at the seacoast just 4km from Nago, so it was a milepost in the old days. Under the tree was a public plaza for villagers; kid's playground, young men's sumo wrestling area, and a place for enjoying cool breezes. Yearly events were also held here and people gathered for drinking, dancing, playing the Sanshin, Okinawan traditional three-stringed instrument.

　After the war, it fell from typhoon damage and second-generation trees were planted in the latter half of the 1970s.

名護　Nago

1917-03-08

Pinus luchuensis Mayr. Liukiu houses and rice field in foreground.

リュウキュウマツ　前方に民家と田んぼ

名護から羽地に向かう宿道の途中、護佐喜宮と呼ばれる拝所がある付近のマツ林。左の茅葺屋根の家々の後ろに穀物の貯蔵庫であった高倉が見える。

On "Sukumichi", the old kingdom highway from Nago to Haneji. Pine forest where the worship shrine, Gosakinomiya is located. You can see Takakura, local raised-floor style granaries at the back of houses.

2017-06-27

今も面影が残る護佐喜宮のマツ林。写真右、奥に延びる道がウィルソンの写真で男たちが立っているかつての宿道。現在は北平和通り（県道71号）と名付けられ、途中で国道58号と合流して仲尾次（羽地）に抜ける。名護市大中2丁目。

The Pine forest surrounds a worship shrine, preserving some appearance of old days. The road with two men standing in Wilson's photo, Sukumichi, became present North Peace Street (Prefectural Route 71) and joins National Route 58 on the way to Haneji. Onaka 2-chome, Nago City.

名護　Nago

1917-03-08

Rice granaries, Sugar mill on left. Nago.

米倉庫　左に製糖場　名護

風通しを良くし湿気を防ぐために礎石の上の柱で支えた高倉。名護近辺、特に羽地は米どころとして知られていた。

Raised floor granaries supported by pillars for ventilation and damp proofing. The Haneji area, north of Nago was well known as a rice-producing region.

1917·03·06

Pinus luchuensis Mayr. 100 ft. tall, girth of trunk from 7-10 ft. *Castanopsis cuspidata* Schott. on right. Mt. Kunchan, Genga

リュウキュウマツ
樹高 30m 幹周 2.1-3m.
右にシイ　国頭山　源河

国頭の山の谷合いでウィルソンが見つけたマツの大木。沖縄本島では最大級のものであった。写真下部に小さく人が写っている。

A fine Pine Wilson found in the mountains of Kunigami. It was the tallest Pine Wilson met on Okinawa main Island. Small figures of persons at the bottom.

Scene 7 屋我地 Yagaji

岬の小海峡を渡り屋我地という小さな島を訪れた。
"I visited the small Island of Yagaji across the neck of the promontory."
E.H.Wilson

干潟の記憶
Remembrance at Tideland

　屋我地島は羽地内海に浮かぶ周囲16kmほどの平坦な島である。現在は島の南端は屋我地大橋で西端はワルミ大橋で、それぞれ沖縄本島と結ばれていて簡単に渡ることができる。そのため、あまり島という感じはしない。しかし、最初の橋ができたのは戦後の1953（昭和28）年で、それまでは完全な孤島で本島への交通と運輸は山原船や刳り舟に頼るしかなかった。

　私は沖縄に来るたびに毎回、この島を訪れている。ウィルソンの撮影場所の検証という理由はあるにしろなぜか、いつも自然と足を向けたくなる場所でもあった。

　Yagaji is a flat island with a circumference of about 16 kilometers floating in Haneji Bay. Today, it is easily accessed from the main island of Okinawa by Yagaji Bridge in the south and Warumi Bridge in the west, so it does not really have the feel of an island. However, until the first bridge was completed in 1953, it was a true island, and for transportation to mainland Okinawa, one had to rely on small local sailboats or dugout canoes.

　Whenever I come to Okinawa, I always visit this island. Even though I could claim that my purpose is to inspect one of Wilson's photograph locations, for whatever reason, my feet just naturally want to point in this direction.

　If you turn your back to the metropolis of Naha and head

大都会那覇を背にひたすら北に向かい、程よいサイズの名護の町から本部半島のつけねを横断し橋を渡るとすぐに、左手に鏡のように静かに広がる湾が見える。屋我地島の南西、アダンが生える海岸にはユウナ（オオハマボウ）の花が時間と共に刻々とその色を変えながら、魔法をかけたような変化を風景に与えていた。湾の水は天候や潮の満ち引きによってさまざまな表情に染まり、動きのない水面に浮かぶいくつもの小島の先に、嘉津宇岳の蒼い稜線が湾の果てを示している。その風景を見ていると、今にも２枚の帆を風に膨らませた船が小さな波を立てて滑るように行き来する姿が見えてきそうな気がしてくる。

　羽地内海はかつて米どころ羽地間切からの貢米を積んだ山原船が仲尾の港から那覇を目指して船出した内海である。ウィルソンはこの港で割り舟を調達して、屋我地島に上陸したのだろうか。上陸地点と思われる浜に、かつてワタサー（渡し役）が一戸あったと島の記録に残っていた。大正期の地図を見ると、当時は島の内部は狭い農道が幾本か走っているだけだったので、この渡し場から島の中心部まで西海岸に沿って馬車を走らせたと想像する。

　橋を作る時に埋め立てが行われたのか、湾に面した砂州の地形は昔と比べて現在は少し異なっているが、海岸沿いのグソー（後世）道には100年前を彷彿とさせる風景がそのまま残っていた。そして、そこから東へ少し入った墨屋原と呼ばれる古い墓地がある所に、ウィルソンが写真に撮ったコバテイシがほとんど変わらぬ枝ぶりで立っている。

　300年以上の時を抱いて、ひたすら墓を守り続けて今に至るその美しい立ち姿に、感動という言葉があまりに陳腐に思えるほどの胸の高鳴りを覚えた。

north from the moderate-sized city of Nago, you'll traverse the Motobu Peninsula where it joins the mainland. Then, just after crossing the bridge, you can see the bay spreading out placidly like a mirror. Along the coast where Screw Pines grow, the flowers of Yuna (Beach Hibiscus) change color as the hours go by, mutating the scenery as if by enchantment. The waters of the bay are steeped in various expressions depending on the weather and the tide, and beyond the small islands that float on that unmoving surface, the blue ridge of Mt. Katsuu marks the edge of the bay. Even today, when I take in this view, it feels as though the shapes of those old small sailboats start to become visible as they come and go and make little waves as they slide by.

　This bay was once called the Kantena Inland Sea and plied by sailboats headed for Naha from the port at Nakao carrying harvest for tribute from the rice-producing district of Haneji. From the harbor, Wilson hired a dugout canoe to reach the southeast side of Yagaji Island. There are records that there used to be one ferry hut (called a watasa) at the beach. At the time, since only narrow farm roads ran to the island's interior, he traveled in his wagon only on the west coast of the island to the center of the village.

　Perhaps due to reclamation when the bridge was made, the shape of the south-west side of the shore has changed a bit in comparison to maps from the past, but the scenery still closely resembles the coastal funeral road (called a guso) where Wilson walked one hundred years ago. Near the old graveyard I discovered a Sea Almond which Wilson photographed still standing with exactly same shape. That beautiful figure in transcending time touched me beyond words.

屋我地　Yagaji

1917-03-07

Terminalia catappa L. 50 ft. tall, girth of trunk 8 ft. Hill beyond dotted with Cycas revoluta Thunb.

モモタマナ（コバテイシ）樹高15.2m 幹周2.4m　遠方にソテツが点在する丘

推定樹齢300〜400年。集落の中心から少し離れた古い墓の近くに立っている。

Estimated present age is between 300 and 400 years old. Near the old graveyard a little way from the center of the village.

2017-03-10

　屋我地島墨屋原。島でいちばん古い横穴式掘抜き墓の隣りに立っているコバテイシは現在も100年前と変わらず存在し、樹高は約16m、幹周は約4.5mと一回り大きくなっている。背景の丘の形状、枝ぶりから、ウィルソンが撮影した木と同じものであると確認できた。フウトウカズラ、アコウ、サクラランなどが太い幹に寄り添うように着生している。

　ウィルソンの写真に写された木の現存を同定できたのは、沖縄では阿嘉島のアカテツと並んでこのコバテイシだけである。

This Sea Almond stands next to the oldest stone burial chamber in Sumiyabara, Yagaji Island. Growing the last 100 years, the present height is about 16m. and girth is about 4.5m. From the shape of the hill in back and shape of branches, I could see this is the same tree Wilson found. Climbing plants and Ficus Superba now cling to the fat trunk.

　This and the Northern Yellow Boxwood tree in Aka island are the only two of Wilson's trees still living.

屋我地　Yagaji

1917-03-07

Pandanus tectorius Soland. With leafless trees of Terminalis catappa L., Garcinia spicata Hook. beneath Pinus luchuensis Mayr.

リュウキュウマツの下に生育するアダン、落葉したモモタマナ（コバテイシ）、フクギ

海岸線の豊かな植生を写している。砂浜にあるのは、ウィルソンを乗せた刳り舟と船頭だろうか。

Shows rich vegetation along the seashore. Small dugout canoe and boatman might have carried Wilson from the opposite shore.

2017-06-27

　橋がなかった戦前まで、屋我地島に渡るのは小さな刳り舟か山原船しかなかった。ウィルソンの写真の奥に茅葺の小屋と井戸が見えることからこの辺りは渡し場であったと思われる。背後のコバテイシは、屋我地島の中心集落を走る道沿いに並ぶ1856年移植の「屋我のコバテイシ並木」の一部とみられる。

　今はモクマオウが繁茂し、同じ位置から並木は見えない。

Before construction of the post war bridge, people used boat or canoe coming and going to Yagaji Island. This place might be the old landing place; there is a small thatch roofed hut and well on the beach in Wilson's photo. Sea Almond trees in the background are part of a lane planted in 1856 along the main street of the village.

Now, it is difficult to see the Sea Almond lane from same position because the Casuaria has grown so thick.

屋我地　Yagaji

Vegetation of Yagaji Island. *Pandanus tectorius* Soland in foreground, *Scaevola koenigii* Vahl. & *Phragmites* sp. On cliffs.

前方にアダン、崖の上にクサトベラとススキなどが生育する屋我地島の植生

屋我地島の南西部海岸の崖の植生。大きな岩の中に洞窟があった。

The vegetation on the cliff on the southwest side of Yagaji Island. There is a cave in the cliff.

1917-03-07

2017·06·27

　写真に写っている一帯の浜道はその昔、グソー（後世）道と呼ばれた野辺送りの道であった。人物の右側のクサトベラが密集する大岩はガンヤームイで、洞窟の中にガン（龕・死者を運ぶ輿）が収められていたと思われる。
　現在、洞窟は生い茂ったアダンで隠されている。

　The narrow beach in Wilson's photo was called Guso-road, the road of the other world. The name of the rock was Ganya-mui and there was a cave a place to store the Gan(portable shrine). When someone died, people carried the body to the cave, put it in the Gan and carried it toward the family graveyard.
　Now, growing Screw Pine hides the cave entrance.

屋我地　Yagaji

1917-03-07

Myoporum bontioides A. Gray.
Height 9 ft.

ハマジンチョウ　樹高2.7m

後方に嘉津宇岳が見える。右遠望に82ページの船着き場の小屋と井戸が写っている。ハマジンチョウは現在、沖縄本島では南城市にしか残っていない。木のそばの人物は園原咲也。

Katsuudake in the background. The boat landing spot and well in P.82 photo are at right in the distance. This species now grows only in Nanjyo City, southeast of Naha. Sakuya Sonohara is standing near the tree.

1917-03-07

島西部、饒平名のマングローブか。当時からオヒルギの純林で知られていた。マングローブの中にたたずむ男性は服装から、県立農学校の訓導（教員）と思われる。

Yohena, west side of Yagaji Island, was a well known spot of the habitat of Black Mangrove. The man standing in the mangrove might be the teacher of Okinawa Prefectural School of Agriculture from his uniform.

Bruguiera gymnorhiza Lam. From 8-12 ft. tall.

オヒルギ　樹高2.4-3.7m

Scene 8 　島人(シマンチュ)と植物　Island Life

琉球の人々の風習や習慣は素朴だ。子供たちの数は多く、幸せそうで屈託がない。
"Manners and customs of Liukiu's people are primitive. Children abound and seem happy, carefree mites."
E.H.Wilson

日常を描く、ウィルソンの眼差し
Wilson's Views of Island's Life

　プラント・ハンターとして、アジアの多くの新種の植物を西洋に紹介したウィルソンだが、日本の旅では植物の発見よりは、むしろ植生調査や生態研究に力点を置いていた。沖縄の探検では、それは自ずと植物と人間との関わりを考察することにもつながった。
　「島の南半分の土地のほとんどが耕作地だった。農業は女たちの労働で成り立っている。主な作物は米、サトウキビ、カライモだった」というウィルソンの描写から、リュウキュウマツやソテツに縁どられた丘の間に広がる田畑や茅葺屋根の農家が点在する村々の牧歌的な風景が想像される。

　Wilson introduced many new Asian plants to the western world as a plant hunter. In addition to this Wilson's goal was to surveys flora and conduct ecological research in Japan. However, his explorations in Okinawa naturally led to inquiry on the relations between plants and people.
　Wilson wrote, "In the southern half of the main island, most of the land is under cultivation. In farming, the Liukiu man depends largely on his women. Rice, sweet potatoes, and sugarcane are the chief crops." From Wilson's description, we can imagine the pastoral scenery of villages dotted with thatched roof farm houses and rice fields bordered by Ryukyu Pines and Cycas spreading out between the hills.
　In those days, industry in Okinawa was centered around

当時の沖縄の産業の中心は農業だった。1912（大正元）年の記録では、農業戸数は総戸数の実に78％を占めている。農業の担い手は、小規模経営農家が圧倒的に多かった。特にサトウキビは、砂糖を租税とする貢糖制が廃止され農民も砂糖の自由販売が許されるようになると、換金植物として盛んに栽培されるようになった。

石油発動機による圧搾機を導入した大規模製糖工場も建設され、砂糖を満載したトロッコ貨車が工場と那覇との間を往復するようになったが、ウィルソンが訪れた頃は、まだほとんどが黒糖を中心とする昔ながらの自家製糖であった。キビ畑のかたわらに牛馬を動力としたサーターヤー（製糖場）があり、砂糖を煮詰める際に燃料とされるソテツが周辺に植えられていた。

また、アダンの葉を編んで帽子や草履を手内職で作る人々の姿もあった。ちなみに、アダン葉で作られた沖縄のパナマ帽は海外にも輸出され、砂糖と同じく重要な県産輸出品となっていた。

互いに向かい合う丘を仰ぎ見れば、陽光を受けて白く輝く墓石群が見え、道脇の大きなガジュマルの影には、御嶽や拝所として祀られた素朴な石の祠が見られた。自然とともに生きる民が、自然を崇拝しながら独自の文化を築いてきた共同体社会の片りんが残っていた時代でもあった。

都心から少し離れた所で営まれていた普通の人々の日常の断片にレンズを向け、ウィルソンがガラス乾板に残した100年前の風景は沖縄の歴史を知るうえで貴重なものだ。時代そのものの息づかいをも写し取り、記録に残そうとしたウィルソンの姿勢の中に、消えゆく時代を愛おしむ眼差しがあった。

agriculture. According to records from 1912, 78% of all households were involved in agriculture, which was overwhelmingly dominated by small-scale farming families. When the sugar-based tax system was abolished and farmers were allowed to freely sell sugar, the cultivation of cash crops led by sugarcane thrived.

Compressors running on petroleum engines were installed in a few large-scale sugar mills being constructed, where trains carrying sugar traveled between mills and Naha, but when Wilson arrived, the sugar industry was still dominated by home operations using traditional methods to produce mostly brown sugar. At the edge of each sugar cane field would be a sugar mill called a sātāyā powered by beasts of burden, and around the perimeter Cycas would be planted for use as fuel when the sugarcane juice was boiled down.

There would be people braiding Screw Pine to make hats and sandals. Incidentally, Panama-style hats made from Screw Pine in Okinawa were exported overseas and, like sugar, became one of the prefecture's important exports.

In Wilson's time, looking up toward hills facing each other, you might see a cluster of gravestones glistening white in the sunshine, and in the shade of a large Banyan tree on the roadside, you could see a simple stone shrine venerated as a sacred site. This was the last glimpse of a communal society whose people had created a distinctive culture living together with nature.

The scenes replicated on glass plate negatives one hundred years ago are precious for studying the history of Okinawa. Attached as he was to an era that was gradually fading away, these scenes are how Wilson captured glimpses of people's daily lives.

島人(シマンチュ)と植物　Island Life

1917-02-26

Liukiu houses. Rice field in foreground. *Ficus retusa* var. *nitida* Miq. in rear. Near Naha.

琉球の民家　前方に田んぼ　後ろにガジュマル　那覇近郊

石垣で囲まれた茅葺屋根の民家。帽子を被った男性は、ウィルソンが現地で雇った手伝いと思われる。

Traditional Ryukyu style thatched house surrounded by stone wall. A local man, Wilson's helper, stands by the house with a hat.

1917-02-26

「住宅は小さな平屋で壁は竹の網代（チヌブ）、屋根は茅葺で、個々の家は、壁や柵で囲まれていた」とウィルソンが記述している。

Wilson wrote "The houses are very small one-storied, constructed of bamboo-wattle sides and thatched roofs. Each is enclosed by a wall or fence."

Trachycarpus excelsus Wendl. 15ft. tall. Liukiu houses on right. *Pinus luchuensis* Mayr. beyond. Near Naha.

シュロ　樹高4.6m　右手に琉球の家
遠方にリュウキュウマツ　那覇近郊

島人（シマンチュ）と植物　Island Life

1917-02-26

Pinus luchuensis Mayr. From 45-50 ft. tall, girth of trunk from 6-8 ft. Among tombs near Naha.

リュウキュウマツ　樹高13.7-15.2m
幹周1.8-2.4m　那覇近郊の墓地

マツに囲まれた丘の上の墓地。那覇近郊ではよく見られた風景だった。

Hill top tombs shaded by Pines. Common scenery in Naha at that time.

1917-03-10

黒々としたマツ林を背景に平葺墓が並ぶ風景。

House shape mausoleums lined on hillside with thick Pine forest in background.

Pinus luchuensis Mayr. forming pure woods. Liukiu Mausoleum in foreground with *Cycas revoluta* Thunb. Near Naha.

リュウキュウマツ　純林を形成　琉球の墓石群とソテツ　　那覇近郊

島人と植物　Island Life

Musa liukiuensis Mak. Cultivated for its fibre which is used for making clothes. Shatan.

リュウキュウバショウ
着物を作る繊維をとるために栽培されている　北谷

別名イトバショウ。戦前まで広く栽培され、葉鞘の繊維で芭蕉布を織り、衣料などに仕上げる作業が普通の家事の一環として営まれていた。

Japanese Fiber Banana was widely planted before the war in Okinawa. Weaving fiber from this plant into cloth used to be ordinary family work.

1917-02-27

Citrus nobilis var. *spontanea* Ito & Matsum. 18 ft. tall, girth of trunk 2 ft., planted. Near Shuri.

クネンボ　樹高 5.5m 幹周 0.6m 栽培種 首里近郊

1917-03-11

かつては民家の庭によく植えられていた東南アジア原産のミカン。「実は苦いが、香りがいい」とウィルソンは口にした感想を残している。

This orange, originally from China, used to be commonly planted around homes. Wilson said "the fruit is bitter but of passable flavor".

島人と植物　Island Life

> *Cycas revoluta* Thunb. Spontaneous on cliffs of coral rock and in Pine woods. Near Naha.
>
> ソテツ　石灰岩の崖の上、松林の中に自生　那覇近郊

救荒植物でもあったソテツは沖縄のあらゆるところで見られ、海岸近くのサンゴ礁や岩に自生し、マツの下生えとして一般的に生育している。

Cycas, an emergency food during famines, is a feature everywhere in Okinawa. It is spontaneous on coral rocks and cliffs near the sea and is a common undergrowth in Pine woods.

1917-02-26

1917·02·26

豊見城村から小禄村の海岸部。アダン帽子作りは沖縄県下のいたるところで盛んになり、重要な輸出品になった。真ん中を走っている黒い線は、輸送中にガラス乾板に入ったひび。

Sea coast of between Tomigusuku Village and Oroku Village. Making hats from Screw Pine was popular throughout Okinawa and became an important export item. The black line in the photo is a crack in the glass plate negative.

Pandanus tectorius Soland. Height 10 ft. Seashore near Naha.

アダン　樹高3m 那覇近郊の海岸部

島人と植物　Island Life

1917-02-25

Native sugar mill. Field of sugarcane in rear. Near Naha.

製糖場（サーターヤー）　後ろにサトウキビ畑　那覇近郊

素朴なサーターグルマ（砂糖圧搾機）を使って働く家族の風景。動力は、左の少年が手綱を持っている小型の馬だった。真玉橋近く。

Family operated small, primitive, Sugar mill used a small horse, led by a boy, for power. Near the Madan Bridge.

1917-03-12

Garcinia spicata Hook. 45-50 ft. tall, girth of trunk from 4-6 ft. School-yard. Naha.

フクギ 樹高 13.7-15.2m 幹周 1.2-1.8m 学校の校庭 那覇

垣花尋常小学校か。石塀の向こうに瓦屋根が見える。現在は、軍港となったため山下町に移転している。

It might be the grounds of Kakinohana school. Beyond the stone wall there are several tiled roofs. The area became the U.S. Navy Port and the school has moved to Yamashita-town.

もうひとつの物語

ウィルソンと琉球を歩いた男
写真の中の園原咲也

　ウィルソンは基本的には一人で旅をし、その土地ごとに協力者を求めた。そして樹木や建造物の大きさを示す尺度として、また旅の思い出に彼らの姿を写真の中に残した。

　沖縄での写真においては、東京から随行した通訳と鹿児島で合流した林業技師の2人以外は、植物採集や撮影機材の運搬などを手伝ったと思われる沖縄在住の研究者や青年たちが写っている。しかし、100年という年月が名前などの手掛かりを得ることを困難にしていた。

　ところが2016年末のことだった。沖縄県立博物館・美術館の学芸員で、企画展「ウィルソンが見た沖縄」担当の一人である園原謙氏から1本の驚きのEメールが届いた。

　「ウィルソンの写真の中に私の祖父を発見しました」。

　写真を1枚ずつ拡大して人物を詳細に見ていくと、確かにそこに沖縄植物学の草分けと言われた園原咲也の若き日の姿があった。窮屈そうにネクタイを締めた咲也は、全部で5枚の写真の中でどこか泰然とした表情を宿してレンズを見つめていた。撮影場所が各地域に散らばっていることから、咲也はウィルソンの沖縄の旅の全行程に同行したと思われる。否、むしろ咲也の案内や段取りに基づき、ウィルソンの旅が企画されたという方が正しいのかもしれない。

　ウィルソンはまた「琉球農政部の職員が最大級の助力をしてくれた」と書き残している。

　私のウィルソンの足跡を追う旅でも、何人もの咲也の思い出を語る人々に出会った。特に山原では「ハブを好んで食べる」「風呂には入らず雨で体を洗う」「いつも植物を口に入れている」など、行き先々でまるで咲也伝説とも言うべきさまざまなエピソードが街角に佇む亡霊のように待ち受けていた。

Another Story—
The Man Who Walked with Wilson
Sakuya Sonohara

In general, Wilson traveled alone and solicited help from locals of the places he visited. He would place these people in his photographs for a sense of scale, to show the size of trees, and also as memories of his travels,

In addition to the interpreter from Tokyo and a forestry engineer from Kagoshima, resident plant researchers and local young men also appear in Wilson's photos in Okinawa. However, the passage of 100 years complicates finding names and other clues to these men.

But the end of 2016 brought a surprise. An astonishing Email arrived from Ken Sonohara, a curator of the Okinawa Prefectural Museum & Art Museum, who was also in charge of the exhibition, "Wilson's Okinawa."

"I found my grandfather in Wilson's photographs." Indeed, when I enlarged each photo and inspected the people within, there was the Okinawan botanical pioneer, Sakuya Sonohara, in his younger days. Despite looking cramped in his necktie, Sakuya maintained a composed countenance as he stared at the lens in a total of five photos. Because the locations of these photos are scattered about different regions, I surmise that Sakuya accompanied Wilson throughout his travels in Okinawa. Or perhaps Wilson's trip was arranged by Sakuya.

Wilson wrote that, "Members of the Okinawa Botany Department have provided top class assistance."

During my own travels in pursuit of Wilson's footsteps, I met many people who reminisced about Sakuya. Like some great legend, particularly in Yanbaru, various tales—how Sakuya liked to eat a venomous snake called the habu, how he washed in the rain instead of taking a bath, and how he was always putting plants in his mouth—awaited me at each turn like loitering spirits.

廃墟から生まれた植物誌

　園原咲也は沖縄生まれではない。雪深い山国、長野県で生まれ木曽山林学校で学んだ後、種子島農林学校の教員として8年余り過ごし、大正元年(1912)に沖縄県の林務技手に推薦され海を渡った。その背景には、この時代ならではの事情があった。当時、沖縄県知事をはじめ県庁の主要職はすべて本土出身者で占められていたが、植物に関してだけは地元の研究者に頼らざるを得なかった。これが面白くなかった県は、本土から専門家を招聘して彼らに対抗させようと目論んだ。しかし役人根性や権威を嫌う性向がある咲也は、県の期待に反して積極的に沖縄の人々と親交を深めていった。

　おそらく県と本人の意向が合致したのだろう。咲也は赴任後まもなくして、名護からさらに36キロ北にある佐手の有林事務所の担当となり、クスノキの造林や林道開設などの仕事の先頭に立った。ウィルソンの案内を命じられたのは、家族と共に人里離れた山原での本格的な暮らしが始まる1か月前、咲也が沖縄の植物研究に本格的に傾倒していく時期だった。

　山原で16年間過ごした後、一旦は県庁勤務となるもすぐに退職。山原に舞い戻った咲也は論文執筆、読書、植物同好会の結成などに力を注ぎ、自由な身を楽しんだ。1939（昭和14）年53歳の時に嘉手納の沖縄県立農林学校の嘱託となり教職に就くが、そこで遭遇したのが1944年10月10日の沖縄大空襲だった。標本をはじめすべての文献資料、日

愛用のカメラで植物の写真を撮る咲也。1959年

Sakuya with his camera 1959.

A Masterpiece Born from the Rubble

　Sakuya Sonohara was not born in Okinawa. He was born in a snowy, mountainous village in Nagano prefecture, and after studying at the Kiso School of Forestry, he spent just over eight years teaching at the Tanegashima School of Agriculture and Forestry before crossing the ocean to Okinawa when he was recommended for the post of forestry engineer in 1912. At work in the background were certain circumstances peculiar to this period. At that time, the governor of Okinawa and major prefectural offices were occupied by people from mainland Japan. Uncomfortable working with local researchers concerning botanical matters, they invited the specialist from the mainland, expecting him to fall in line with their policies. However, it was in Sakuya's nature to loathe bureaucratic authority, and contrary to the prefecture's expectations he actively cultivated deep friendships with Okinawan people.

　Perhaps because of this difference in outlook, shortly after Sakuya's appointment the prefecture sent him to the far north to be in charge of the public forest administration office in Sate, 36km north of Nago. There Sakuya involved himself with planting conifers and building mountain routes. When he was charged with guiding Wilson, Sakuya and his family had just settled in that remote area a month earlier, and he was beginning to genuinely devote himself to research the flora of Okinawa.

　After spending sixteen years in the mountains of Yanbaru, he was reassigned to work in the prefectural office in Naha but soon retired. He enjoyed his freedom and poured his energy into academic writing, reading, and formation of a botany circle. In 1939, at the age of 53, he took up a part-time teaching position at the Okinawa

記などが那覇の宿舎と共に焼失し、身ひとつで弾を避けながら山原の山中に避難した。

戦後、マラリアに罹り痩せこけた状態の咲也の姿が米軍が設けた収容所で発見された。生きる気力を失った咲也を蘇らせたのは、米国民政府のSIRI（琉球諸島科学調査）スタッフだったエグバード・H・ウォーカーに協力して、沖縄の植物調査をする事業への参加だった。戦争直後の最悪の条件下で、頭の中にあった知識と経験だけを頼りに咲也は２人の後輩と共に焦土となった沖縄を駆け回った。資料がないため白紙から始められたこの仕事は、やがて『沖縄植物誌』に結実され、以降の沖縄植物研究の礎となる大著となった。

「沖縄諸島の植物は十分には研究されていない。多くの仕事が残されている」という言葉と共に沖縄を後にしたウィルソンだが、そのやり残した仕事を引き継いだのが咲也だったとも言えるだろう。

多和田眞淳、天野鉄夫との共著、ウォーカー編集による『沖縄植物誌』。琉球列島米国民政府による出版　1952年

'Flora of Okinawa' co-written with Shinjyu Tawada and Tetsuo Amano edited by E.H.Waker published by United States Civil Administration of Ryukyu Islands in 1952.

米国領事館領事よりウォーカー氏の本『沖縄・南琉球諸島植物誌』を受け取る咲也、国頭村役場村長室にて　1970年

The U.S. Consul passed to Sakuya the new edition of 'Flora of Okinawa and the Southern Ryukyu Islands" written with E.H,Walker at Kunigami village office in 1970.

Prefectural Agricultural School in Kadena. The air raids of Okinawa occurred on October 10th, 1944. His valuable specimens and all of his written material and diaries were destroyed. He could take nothing with him as he dodged bullets and fled back to the mountains of Yanbaru.

After the war, he was found at an internment camp underweight and suffering from malaria. It was participation in a survey of Okinawan flora in cooperation with Egbert H. Walker, one of the staff of SIRI (the U.S. Scientific Investigations in the Ryukyu Islands) that renewed his will to live. In unfathomable post-war conditions, he relied on the knowledge and experience stored in his head as he roamed together with two junior colleagues over the scorched earth that Okinawa had become. This work, which started with nothing but blank paper since there were no remaining documents, reached fruition as the voluminous work entitled, "Flora of Okinawa," and served as the cornerstone for subsequent research on Okinawan flora.

Wilson took his leave of Okinawa with the words, "The flora of the Okinawan archipelago has not been studied enough. There remains much work to be done." It can be said that it was Sakuya who took over this work.

The Legendary Old Man

Sakuya spent his later years as a lecturer, diligently coaching his juniors at the Prefectural Hokubu Agricultural School in Nago till 89 years old. Even now, the figure of Sakuya—looking the part of a mountain sage as he heads off into the hills carrying his worn-out gray rucksack with nothing but pruning shears and frying pan inside—has not departed from the memories of the people of Yanbaru. With affection and esteem, they call him tanmē, grandfather, in the dialect of Okinawa. Such

園原タンメー

その後、咲也は89歳まで名護の沖縄県立北部農林学校の講師として後進の指導に励んだ。剪定鋏とフライパンだけが入ったぼろぼろの灰色のリュックを背負って山に入る仙人のような咲也の姿は、今なお山原の人々の記憶から離れない。人々は親しみと尊敬を込めて、沖縄の方言で祖父を意味する「タンメー」と彼を呼ぶ。沖縄人以上に沖縄人として生きた咲也の一生だった。

ウィルソンと咲也が交錯した100年前の日に私の想像は飛ぶ。小学校卒業から自力で植物学を学びプラント・ハンターとして世界の頂点に立った41歳のウィルソンと、沖縄での自分の立ち位置を見極めようと模索していた31歳の咲也は、いったいどんな時間を分かち合ったのだろうか。

名誉欲がなく純粋な自然人で、植物研究に生涯をかけた2人は共通点が多い。山を愛し、人を愛し、酒を愛した。1日の探索が終わった夕べ、宿で採集した植物を分類、乾燥させながら共有された時間の片隅に、泡盛とウィスキーが仲良く並ぶ光景が目に浮かぶ。

ウィルソンは第二次大戦の勃発を知ることなく、1930年ボストン郊外での交通事故で54歳の生涯を突然、終えた。敗戦の廃墟から立ち上がった咲也は、沖縄が日本に復帰する日を見て死にたいと願い、その言葉通り沖縄の施政権がアメリカから日本に返還されてから9年後の1981年、山原の自宅で95歳の天寿を全うした。

晩年の咲也。94歳 1979年
Sakuya at 94.1979.

トレードマークのリュックを背負って山を歩く咲也。
1959年

Sakuya, walking in the mountain with his trademark rucksack.

was the life of Sakuya, who lived the life of an Okinawan as much any native.

I can only imagine what the day must have been like, one hundred years ago, when Wilson and Sakuya first crossed paths; Wilson, who at age 41 had stood at the summit of the plant hunting world after taking it upon himself to study botany ever since finishing elementary school, and Sakuya, now 31, who had come to Okinawa to develop his path in life. What sort of times must they have shared together?

There was much in common between two men of genuine, natural character, who felt no hunger for fame, and who dedicated their lives to botanical research. They loved the mountains, they loved humans, they loved alcohol. I can picture them in the evenings, after the end of the day's exploits, classifying and drying the plants they had collected while awamori and whiskey stood cordially at the ready.

Wilson was not around for the outbreak of World War II, for his life ended abruptly in a traffic accident in the suburbs of Boston in 1930 when he was 54. Sakuya rebuilt his life after the devastation, hoping he would live long enough to see Okinawa returned to Japan, finally passing away in 1981, 9 years after the reversion, at the ripe old age of 95.

（文中、園原咲也の年齢は満年齢で計算）

ウィルソンの沖縄踏査地図

　今からちょうど100年前、1917（大正６）年の２月25日から３月13日までの17日間、ウィルソンは沖縄に滞在し、精力的に写真撮影と植物採集に身を投じた。

　那覇を拠点に主に客馬車を使って宿道をたどり北谷、首里、中城、名護を周り、また船を雇って慶良間諸島と屋我地島にも足を延ばした。先島諸島にも訪れたかったようだか、定期船がなくまた、十分な時間も確保できないため諦めざるを得なかったのが心残りだったようだ。

　沖縄を訪れて植物を採集した西洋人はウィルソンが初めてではない。19世紀になってからバジル・ホール、ウィリアム・ビーチ、さらには米国海軍ペリー提督の艦隊に同行した複数のプラント・ハンターなどが記録を残している。彼らの軌跡に触れながら、ウィルソンは言う。「琉球の植物は今日の西洋の標本館では非常に数が少ない。私はできうる限り多くの乾燥標本を集めたい」

　ウィルソンの関心は特に、リュウキュウマツとハイネズという琉球固有の針葉樹の研究をすることにあった。マツは自生、植栽を問わず、いたるところで目にすることができ、ハイネズは慶良間諸島と屋我地島で観察できた。また、新たに発見し自身の名を付けて命名した植物もいくつかあった。

　沖縄では雨の多い時期であったが、「全般的に天候に恵まれ、成果のある旅ができた」という言葉で成功裏に終わった旅を後に述懐している。

ウィルソンの来沖を伝える1917（大正６）年２月26日の琉球新報記事。「学術研究のため昨日来県せり」とある。

A newspaper article that reported Wilson's visit to Okinawa, Ryukyu Simpo Newspaper, Feb. 26, 1917. It reported, "Prof. Ernest Wilson visited our prefecture for academic investigation yesterday."

Wilson's Route in Okinawa

　One hundred years ago, for seventeen days spanning from February 25th through March 13th 1917, Wilson sojourned in Okinawa, setting out energetically to take photographs and collect specimens.

　From his base in Naha, Wilson used mostly horse-drawn wagons to travel around Chatan, Shuri, Nakagusuku, and Nago, and he also hired boats to extend his explorations to the Kerama Islands and Yagaji Island. Apparently, he had further hoped to visit the Sakishima Islands, but with no regularly operating passage and no guarantee of enough time, he regretted abandoning this opportunity.

　Wilson was not the first Westerner to visit Okinawa and collect plants. In the 19th century, there are records of Captain Basil Hall, William Beechey, and several plant hunters that traveled with Commodore Perry's naval fleet from the United States. While covering the paths of these others, Wilson commented, "Liukiu plants are today rare in western herbaria. I want to collect as many dried specimens as possible."

　Wilson was especially interested in studying the Ryukyu Pine and the Shore Juniper (Juniperus conferta), the two endemic conifers in the Ryukyu islands. He was able to find Pine trees everywhere, both wild and cultivated, and he was able to observe the Shore Juniper in the Kerama Islands and on Yagaji Island. He also discovered several plants which he named for himself.

　Although it was a rainy time of year in Okinawa, after completing his journey Wilson recollected, "The weather on the whole was fine and I have pleasure in reporting a successful trip."

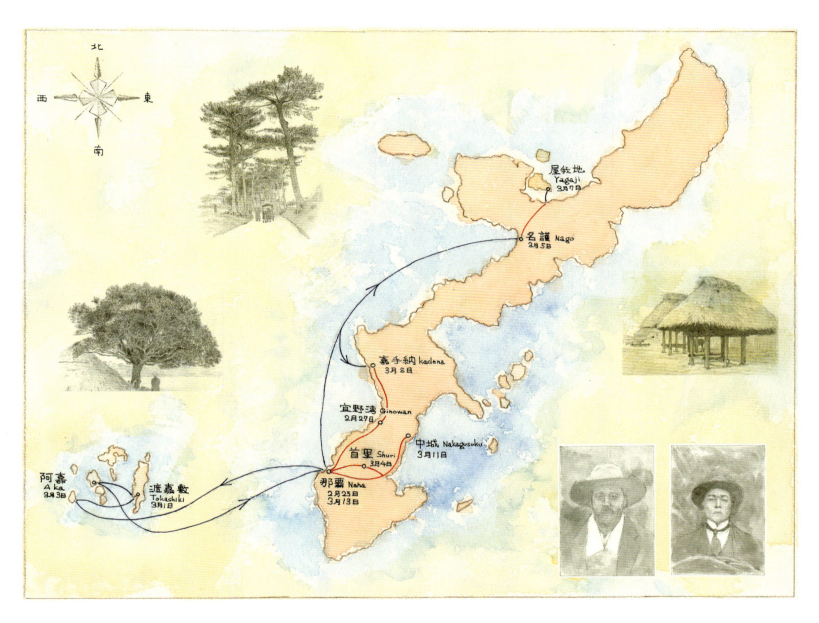

ウィルソン手書きのフィールド・ノート。2ページから19ページの#8000〜#8189までは1917年2月24日から3月12日にかけて沖縄で採集した植物名・採集場所が記入されている。

Field notebook of Wilson in his handwriting. He described the plants' scientific names and collecting places in Okinawa from page2 to page19, Feb24~Mar.12, 1917.

100年後のために記録に残す

　ウィルソンは沖縄のフィールドで59枚の写真を撮り、100種以上に及ぶ約600点の乾燥さく葉標本を採集した。写真はハーバード大学アーノルド樹木園の資料庫に、標本のほとんどは同大学標本館に保存されていた。

　何より、19世紀末に商品化されたばかりのカメラを活用し、標本やスケッチに頼ってきたそれまでのプラント・ハンターと異なり、植物が自然に生育する姿を記録したウィルソンの功績は大きい。

　イギリスのサンダーソン社が開発した最新鋭のフィールド・カメラを使って、乳剤を塗ったガラス乾板に感光させ写し取られた画像は実に鮮明で美しい。考え抜かれた構図の美しさ、全体に流れる気品の高さなど、同時代に撮られた写真のなかでも傑出しているといっていいだろう。

　旅を続ける中で、ウィルソンはカメラの新しい可能性にいち早く気がついたと思われる。単なる事実を記録するという道具としての価値だけではなく、撮影者の思いを伝える媒体にもなり得るということだった。それはまた、ひとりの表現者へとウィルソンの視点を変えることにもつながっていった。

　現代の私たちがそれを見る時、撮影者が残した私たちへの強いメッセージを改めて想起させられる。

　本著では、ウィルソンが使用した15.5cm×20cmのガラス乾板にできるだけ近い大きさで写真を掲載した。

Records for 100 Years Later

Wilson took 59 field-shots and collected 600 dried specimens representing over one hundred plant species in Okinawa. The photographs are stored in the archives of Arnold Arboretum and almost all of the specimens are preserved in the Herbarium at Harvard University.

Prominent among Wilson's tremendous achievements was utilization of the camera, which had become commercially available at the end of the 19th century, to record living figures of plants in nature in a way that conveys more than mere specimens and sketches.

He used a state-of-the-art field camera developed by Sanderson & Company in England, and the images reproduced on the glass plates coated in emulsion are absolutely vivid and beautiful. The beauty of his thoughtful compositions and the level of elegance that flows throughout make Wilson's photographs stand out from others of the period.

It is thought that, while on his travels, Wilson soon realized the new potential of the camera. Beyond the value as a tool for recording reality, this medium could also convey the sentiments of the photographer. Through this work Wilson would change his viewpoint into a sort of story teller beyond simple plant hunter or botanist.

When we of the present look at these photographs, they once more call to mind the powerful message that the photographer left for us.

Photographs in this book are reproduced as close as possible to the original size of Wilson's 15.5cm by 20.5cm glass plates.

ウィルソンが沖縄での撮影に使用したのと同型の「サンダーソン・カメラ」（©日本カメラ博物館JCII CAMERA MUSEUM）

The Sanderson Camera of the same type that Wilson used for photography in Japan.

もし写真や標本で記録を残さなかったならば、100年後にはその多くは消えてなくなってしまうだろう。

E.H.ウィルソン

"If we do not get such records of them in the shape of photographs and specimens, a hundred years hence many will have disappeared entirely."

E H. Wilson

　まるで、たった今、採集したばかりのようなみずみずしい色合いを保っているさく葉標本の現物を間近に見た時、これらを作成、保管しながら旅を続け、厳重に梱包し、自ら管理して蒸気船で一緒にボストンに帰国したウィルソンの努力を思う。そして、その努力は損なわれることなく100年という年月の間、適切な環境で管理され続けてきた。

　標本もまた、学術的な面だけでなく、歴史を記録するドキュメンタリーとして貴重なものである。

When I observed the actual specimens at Harvard University Herbaria that still hold on to vibrant tints of color as if they had only just been collected, I admired the efforts of Wilson, who created and safeguarded these specimens as he continued his travels, packing them securely and personally caring for them as he returned by steamship to Boston. I also admired the stance of the herbarium, which has continued to curate these specimens in a suitable environment for the span of one hundred years, so that Wilson's efforts would not be wasted.

　These samples are not only interesting from an academic perspective, but they are also precious documents of the past.

1917年と1918年の沖縄、伊豆大島、小笠原、朝鮮半島、台湾の探検で集めた植物標本。ボストン、アーノルド樹木園フェンネル管理棟1階の標本アトリウムにてウィルソンが撮影（1919年4月）

E.H. Wilson's collection of herbarium specimens of Okinawa, Izuoshima, Ogasawara, Korea, Taiwan made in 1917 and 1918. Photographed by Wilson in the atrium, Ist floor, herbarium wing, Hunnewell Administration Building at Arnold Arboretum in Boston. April 1919.

フクギ
Garcinia spicata Hook.

ソテツ
Cycas revoluta Thunb.

©Gray Herbarium and Herbarium of the Arnold Arboretum of Harvard University, Cambridge, MA. USA.

チーム・ウィルソン　Team Wilson　（敬称略・50音順）（In alphabetic order）

赤井賢成　Kensei Akai
［植物監修］
現在のプラントハンター／（一財）沖縄美ら島財団
Plant Adviser. Present Plant Hunter. Curator & Researcher of Okinawa Churashima Foundation.

垣花武一　Takeichi Kakinohana
［阿嘉島歴史情報提供］
語り部／阿嘉島在住
Provided historical information of Kerama Islands. Historical Reciter.
Resident of Akajima.

垣花　佑　Yu Kakinohana
［阿嘉島ロケーション協力］
座間味村教育委員会
Located Wilson's sites in Aka Island. Zamami Village Education Board.

我那覇　博　Hiroshi Ganaha
［垣花町ロケーション協力］
アメリカン・リジョン相談員
Located Wilson's sites in Kakinohana Town. Advisor of American Region.

岸本　林　Hayashi Kishimoto
［屋我地島ロケーション協力］
名護のインディ・ジョーンズ／名護市文化財保存調査委員
Located Wilson's sites in Yagaji Island. Indiana Jones in Nago.
Nago City Cultural Heritage Preservation and Research Committee.

具志堅千恵子　Chieko Gushiken
［現在写真撮影］
琉球新報写真記者
Photographed current Wilson's sites. Photojournalist of Ryukyu Shimpo.

島袋徳正　Norimasa Shimabukuro
［園原咲也情報提供］
園原タンメーの愛弟子／植物研究家／名護在住
Provided Sakuya Sonohara's legendary stories. Plant Researcher. Devoted follower of Sonohara tanmē.
Resident of Nago.

城間恒宏　Tsunehiro Shiroma
［豊見城周辺ロケーション協力］
生物教師／沖縄県教育庁文化財課
Located Wilson's sites in Tomigusuku Area. Teacher of Biology. Okinawa Prefecture Cultural Properties Division, Okinawa Education Bureau.

園原　繁　Shigeru Sonohara
［園原咲也情報提供］
園原咲也の子息／元国頭村教育長／辺土名在住
The son of Sakuya Shinohara. Former Superintendent of Education in Kunigami Village. Resident of Hentona.

知念勝美　Katsumi Chinen
［渡嘉敷島植物情報提供］
県立高校教諭
Provided the plant information of Tokashiki Island. Teacher of Prefectural High School, Uruma City.

知花史尚　Fuminao Chibana
［沖縄県植物情報提供］
ナチュラリスト／県立商業高校教頭
Provided the plant information of Okinawa. Naturalist. Vice-principal of Prefectural Commercial High School, Naha City.

寺田仁志　Jinshi Terada
［南西諸島植生情報提供］
南方放浪家／文化庁調査員／屋久島出身
Provided general flora of South-West Islands. Wanderer of Southern area in Japan. Researcher of the Agency for Cultural Affairs. Born in Yakushima.

チーム・ウィルソン　Team Wilson　(敬称略・50音順) (In alphabetic order)

当山昌直　Masanao Toyama
[沖縄歴史情報提供]
島歩き屋 / 生物文化研究者 / 沖縄県教育庁文化財課
Provided general historical information of Okinawa. Islands Watcher. Okinawa Prefecture Cultural Properties Division, Okinawa Education Bureau.

濱川　靖　Yasushi Hamakawa
[奥武山ロケーション協力]
生物教師 / 沖縄県教育庁文化財課
Located Wilson's sites in Onoyama, Naha. Teacher of Biology. Staff of the Okinawa Prefecture Cultural Properties Division. Okinawa Education Bureau.

樋口謙一　Kenichi Higuchi
[情報提供＆サポート]
コピーライター / 首里在住
Provided various kind of information and support of research. Copy Writer. Resident of Shuri.

平敷兼哉　Kenya Heshiki
[宜野湾街道ロケーション協力]
宜野湾市立博物館学芸員
Located Wilson's sites in Old Ginowan Avenue. Curator of Ginowan City Museum.

外間政明　Masaaki Hokama
[那覇市歴史情報提供]
那覇市歴史博物館
Provided historical information of Naha City. Senior curator of Naha City Historical Museum. Naha.

松島弘明　Hiroaki Matsushima
[首里ロケーション協力]
古都首里探訪会会員 / 沖縄県俳句協会会員 / 首里在住
Located Wilson's sites in Shuri. Member of the Old Capital Tour in Shuri Association and Okinawa Haiku Association. Resident of Shuri.

宮平友介　Yusuke Miyahira
[比謝矼歴史情報提供]
歴史研究家 / 嘉手納町教育委員会民俗資料室
Provided historical information about Hijya bridge area. Historical Researcher. Kadena Museum of History, Kadena Town Education Board.

村田尚史　Naofumi Murata
[名護ロケーション協力]
熱心なウィルソニアン / 名護博物館学芸員
Located Wilson's sites in Nago City. Devoted Wilsonian. Curator of Nago Museum.

吉田朝啓　Chokei Yoshida
[首里歴史情報提供]
医師 / 首里在住
Provided historical information and experiences of Shuri. Doctor. Resident of Shuri.

米田英明　Hideaki Yoneda
[渡嘉敷島ロケーション協力]
琉球新報渡嘉敷村通信員
Located Wilson's sites in Tokashiki Island. Correspondent of Tokashiki Island, Ryukyu Shimpo.

沖縄とウィルソンのついての情報、記憶を提供して下さったすべての方々に心から感謝申し上げます。
I am sincerely grateful that I could meet all the people who provided information and memories about Okinawa and Wilson.

サブチーム・屋久島　制作協力
Subteam Yakushima. Special thanks in production of this book.

ジェニファー・ルー　Jennifer Lue [英訳アシスト] 山岳ガイド
English translation assist. Mountain guide.

黒飛　淳　Atsushi Kurotobi [ウィルソンの踏査地図挿画] 画家
Illustrated the map of Wilson's Route in Okinawa. Artist.

ウィリアム・ブラワー　William Brouwer [装丁デザイン / 翻訳編集] 建築家・造形デザイナー
Cover design, book design concept and translation editing. Architectural designer & builder.

後記

　ウィルソンが見た1917年の沖縄は、各分野でのヤマト化が急速に進むと同時に琉球の歴史的特性が失われていく過渡期であり、また沖縄戦の悲劇へとつながる布石が打たれつつあった時代でもあった。

　この本は琉球新報の連載（2017年1月～12月）をベースに、沖縄の次の世紀について考えるひとつのきっかけになればという思いを込めて書き上げた。ウィルソンが写真の中に封じ込めた100年前の数々の物語と未来へのメッセージを感じとっていただけたら幸いである。

　過重な米軍基地負担という出口の見えない問題を抱えて苦悶する現代の沖縄で、「ウチナーンチュである」という強いアイデンティティを持つ方々と共有させていただいた時間はかけがえのないものだった。多くのことを学ぶ機会を与えてくださった方々に心から感謝したい。

　最後に、いつも私の理解者でいて下さった琉球新報の米倉外昭文化部長に感謝の言葉を捧げたい。

2017年9月
屋久島にて　古居智子

Author's Note

　The Okinawa Wilson observed in 1917 was a transition period when Ryukyu's historical features were starting to vanish rapidly, laying the foundations for the future tragedy of World War Ⅱ.

　I wrote this book, based on a series of articles in Ryukyu Shimpo(Jan.2017~Dec.2017), hoping that an understanding of changes in the past 100 years may help to think about a better next century for Okinawa.

　In the present Okinawa, struggling with the burden of the U.S. military bases, I shared valuable time with people who have strong identities as Okinawans. They gave me the chance to learn many things.

　Also, I deeply appreciate Gaisho Yonekura, journalist of Ryukyu Shimpo, who always encouraged me.

September 2017, Yakushima
Tomoko Furui

謝辞　Acknowledgements

ハーバード大学アーノルド樹木園　Arnold Arboretum of Harvard University
ハーバード大学標本館 Harvard University Herbaria
沖縄県立博物館・美術館 Okinawa Prefectural Museum and Art Museum
一般財団法人沖縄美ら島財団 Okinawa Churashima Foundation
公益財団法人屋久島環境文化財団 Yakushima Environmental Foundation
沖縄県教育庁　Okinawa Education Bureau　／沖縄県教育委員会 Okinawa Pefectural Board of Education
那覇市歴史博物館 Naha City Museum of History
宜野湾市立博物館 Ginowan City Museum　／　名護博物館 Nago Museum
那覇市文化協会 Naha City Cultural Association　／　古都首里探訪会 Old Capital Shuri Tour Association
那覇市 Naha City　／ 豊見城市 Tomigusuku City ／ 名護市　Nago City
嘉手納町 Kadena Town　／ 読谷村 Yomitan Village ／ 座間味村 Zamami Village
渡嘉敷村 Tokashiki Village　／ 国頭村 Kunigami Village

本書中の植物学名は、ウィルソンの表記のまま使用。
Scientific names in this book are those used by Wilson.

主な参考文献　References

日本文資料　Japanese Sources

金城正篤他『沖縄県の百年　県民100年史』山川出版社、2005年
大田朝敷『沖縄県政50年』琉球新報社、1932年
東恩納寛惇『南島風土記（沖縄・奄美・大島地名辞典）』沖縄財団、1950年
宮城栄昌・高宮廣衛『沖縄歴史地図 歴史編』柏書房、1983年
新里金福・大城立裕　琉球新報社編『沖縄の百年　第一巻～第三巻』太平出版社、1969年
佐久田繁編『沖縄の歴史　明治・大正・昭和の百年』月刊沖縄社、1972年
沖縄県文化振興会公文書管理部史料編集室『概説　沖縄の歴史と文化』沖縄県教育委員会、2000年
上里隆史『新聞投稿に見る百年前の沖縄』原書房、2016年
上里隆史『目からウロコの琉球・沖縄史』ボーダーインク、2007年
上里隆史『あやしい！目からウロコの琉球・沖縄史』ボーダーインク、2014年
上里隆史『海の王国・琉球「海域アジア」屈指の交易国家の実像』洋泉社、2012年
琉球新報社編『写真集　むかし沖縄』琉球新報社、1990年
琉球新報社編『絵はがきにみる沖縄　明治・大正・昭和』琉球新報社、1993年
琉球新報社編『新琉球史 近代・現代編』琉球新報社、1992年
沖縄歴史教育研究会 新城俊昭『教養講座 琉球・沖縄史』編集工房東洋企画、2014年
ジョージ.H.カーン 山口栄鉄訳『沖縄　島人の歴史』勉誠出版、2014年
沖縄県教育委員会『沖縄県歴史の道調査報告書』沖縄県教育委員会、1988年
R.ゴールドシュミット 平良研一・中村哲勝訳『大正時代の沖縄』琉球新報社、1981年
海ална文彦『おきなわ懐かし写真館　復帰前へようこそ』ゆうな社、2012年
新垣光勇『ウチナーグチ資料集』郷土出版、2007年
那覇市企画部市史編集室編『那覇市史 通史編第2巻 近代史』那覇市役所、1974年
那覇市企画部市史編集室編『琉球処分百年記念出版写真集 激動の記録 那覇百年のあゆみ』那覇市、1980年
豊見城市『豊見城村史』豊見城市、1964年
豊見城市史　第二巻民俗編』豊見城市、2008年
宜野湾市史編集委員会『宜野湾市史別冊 写真集ぎのわん』宜野湾市教育委員会、1991年
高良倉吉『琉球王国』岩波新書、1993年
古都首里探訪会編著『王都首里見て歩き 御地と全19町ガイド＆マップ』2016年
野々村孝男『首里城を救った男 阪谷良之進・柳田菊造の軌跡』ニライ社、1999年
上里隆史『人をあるく 尚氏と首里城』吉川弘文館、2016年
『首里城』毎日新聞社、1993年
渡嘉敷村史編集委員会『渡嘉敷村史 通史編』渡嘉敷村役場、1990年
渡嘉敷村史編集委員会『渡嘉敷村史 資料編』渡嘉敷村役場、1987年
座間味村史編集委員会『座間味村史 上巻・中巻・下巻』座間味村役場、1989年
曽野綾子『ある神話の背景　沖縄・渡嘉敷の集団自決』PHP研究所、1992年
「5000年の記憶」編集委員会編『5000年の記憶 名護市民の歴史と文化』名護市史編さん室、2000年
名護市史編さん委員会『写真集 名護-ひとびとの100年』名護市役所、1990年
名護市史編さん委員会『名護市史資料2 戦前新聞集成1』名護市役所、1984年
名護市史編さん委員会『名護市史資料3 戦前新聞集成2』名護市役所、1985年
『第17回企画展　屋我地-その歴史と自然-』名護博物館、2000年
比謝矼誌編集員会『比謝矼誌』比謝矼公民館、1995年
手塚好幸編著『沖縄近代林業の父 園原咲也と木曽山林学校』2010年
田井寄茂編『季刊文芸誌 脈 第39号 特集園原咲也』脈発行所、1990年
天野鉄夫『新聞から見た園原咲也先生の素顔』OKタイプセンター、1974年
『うむさ 第9号 園原咲也先生追悼特集』北部農林同窓会那覇支部、1981年
『ウォーカー博士が見た沖縄の原風景～米国植物学者の偉業と写真で綴る1950年代の沖縄』ウォーカー博士展実行委員会、2001年
團伊玖磨監修『沖縄・薩南の島々 にっぽん島の旅⑤』中央公論社、1984年
『美しい日本⑫　沖縄・小笠原の自然』世界文化社、1981年
牧野和春編『九州・沖縄 巨樹名木巡り』牧野出版、1991年
城間朝教編著『沖縄の自然植物誌カラー自然シリーズ⑦』新星図書、1977年
沖縄県『天然記念物緊急調査　植生図・主要動植物地図』文化庁、1976年
大川智史・林将之『琉球の樹木　奄美・沖縄～八重山の亜熱帯植物図鑑』文一総合出版、2016年
赤嶺政信監修『沖縄の神と食の文化』青春出版社、2003年
『写真集沖縄 失われた文化財と民俗』那覇出版社、1984年
国立歴史民俗博物館編『琉球弧-海洋をめぐるモノ・人、文化-』岩田書院、2012年
岡本太郎『沖縄文化論-忘れられた日本』中央公論社、1996年
島尾敏雄『ヤポネシア序説』創樹社、1977年
九学会連合沖縄調査委員会『沖縄-自然・文化・社会』弘文堂、1976年
大庭邦彦・長志球絵・小林知子『Jr.日本の歴史⑥大日本帝国の時代』小学館、2011年
『太陽コレクション地図　江戸・明治・現在』平凡社、1977年
佐藤　信・吉田伸之『新大系日本史6 都市社会史』山川出版社、2001年
東京国立博物館編『海上の道 沖縄の歴史と文化』読売新聞社、1992年
豊見山和行・高良倉吉編『琉球・沖縄と海上の道』吉川弘文館、2005年
ラヴ・オーシュリ編著・上原正稔編著・訳『青い目が見た「大琉球」』ニライ社、1987年
上原兼善『鎖国と密貿易 - 薩摩藩の琉球密貿易』八重岳書房、1981年
高良倉吉『琉球の時代 - 大いなる歴史像を求めて』筑摩書房、2012年
外間守善『沖縄の歴史と文化』中央公論新社、1986年
司馬遼太郎『街道をゆく6 沖縄・先島への道』朝日新聞社、1978年
大江健三郎『沖縄ノート』岩波新書、1970年
NHKスペシャル取材班『NHKスペシャル　沖縄戦全記録』新日本出版社、2016年
大田昌秀『沖縄の民衆意識』新泉社、1995年
大田昌秀『沖縄の決断』朝日新聞社、2000年
大田昌秀『沖縄のこころ―沖縄戦と私』岩波新書、1972年
毎日新聞社編『大正という時代「100年前」に日本の今を探る』毎日新聞社、2012年
新崎盛暉『沖縄同時代史第二巻 琉球弧の視点から 1978-1982』凱風舎、1992年
隅谷三喜男『日本の歴史22　大日本帝国の試練』中公文庫、1974年
海野弘『1914年　100年前から今を考える』平凡社、2014年
井上寿一『第一次世界大戦と日本』講談社、2014年
山口栄鉄『チェンバレンの琉球・沖縄発見』芙蓉書房出版、2016年
M.C.ペリー・F.L.ホークス他　宮崎嘉子訳『ペリー提督日本遠征記＜上＞＜下＞』角川書店、2014年
佐野眞一『沖縄 だれにも書かれたくなかった戦後史＜上＞＜下＞』集英社、2011年
大城立裕『小説 琉球処分 上・下』講談社、2010年
白幡洋三郎『プラントハンター』講談社、2005年
F.キングドン-ウォード 塚谷裕一訳『植物巡礼-プラント・ハンターの回想』岩波文庫、1999年
T.ホイットル『プラント・ハンター物語 植物を世界に求めて』八坂書房、1983年
琉球新報　1917.2.25～3.12

英文資料　English Sources

E. H. Wilson. 1917. *Correspondence 1917 Mar 21-Dec.31*. Archive of Arnold Arboretum, Harvard University, Boston.
E. H. Wilson. *Field Notes on collected plants and seed feb.1917-Mar.1975*. Archive of Arnold Arboretum, Harvard University, Boston.
E. H. Wilson. 1917. Ryukyu "February 25-March 1917." Archive of Arnold Arboretum, Harvard University, Boston.
E. H. Wilson. 1917. *Kerama Islands*. Archive of Arnold Arboretum, Harvard University, Boston.
E. H. Wilson. 1920. *The Liukiu Islands and Their Lingneous Vegetation*. Journal of the Arnold Arboretum Volume 1 January, 1920 Nomber 3. Archive of Arnold Arboretum, Harvard University, Boston.
George H. Kerr 1958. *Okinawa~The History of Island People*. Charles E. Tuttle Company, Rutland, Vermont, Tokyo.
E. H. Wilson. 1891. *The Romance of Our Trees*. Cornell University Library, New York.
E. H. Wilson. 1913. *A Naturalist in Western China-With vasculum, camera, and Gun*. Cambridge Library Collection, Cambridge University Press.
E. H. Wilson. 1917. *Aristocrats of the Garden*. Doubleday, Page & Company.
E. H. Wilson. 1927. *Plant Hunting, Volume I & II*. University Press of the pacific Honolulu, Hawaii.
E. H. Wilson. 1930. *Aristocrats of the Trees*. The Stratford Company. London.
Edward I. Farrington. 1931. *Ernest H. Wilson Plant Hunter*. The Stratford Company. London.
Alfred Rehder. *Ernest Henry Wilson*. Archive of Arnold Arboretum, Harvard University, Boston.
Richard A. Howard. *E.H.Wilson as a Botanist*. Archive of Arnold Arboretum, Harvard University, Boston.
Alice M. Coats. 1969. *The Quest for Plants: A History of the Horticultural Explorers*. Studio Vista Limited, London.
Roy W Briggs. 1993. *'Chinese' Wilson A Life of Ernest H Wilson 1876-1930*. HMSO Publicaions, London.
Michael Tyler-Whittle. 1970. *The Plant Hunters*. London
Toby Musgrave, Chris Gardner, Will Musgrave. 1998. *The Plant Hunters*. Seven Dials, Cassell & Co. London
Carolyn Fry. 2009. *The Plant Hunters -The Adventures of The World's Greatest Botanical Explorers*. Carlton Books Limited, London

著者 Author

古居　智子（ふるい　ともこ）

大阪生まれ。北海道大学卒。米国ボストンでジャーナリストとして活躍後、1994年屋久島に移住。2001年ＮＰＯ法人屋久島エコ・フェスタを設立。環境保護活動に励みながら、日本と欧米の交流史や屋久島の歴史、文化、自然などをテーマに執筆活動を続けている。2011年からウィルソンの調査を開始。資料の発掘と取材執筆に情熱を注ぐ。
http://www.t-furui.jp/

Tomoko Furui

Born in Osaka. Graduated from Hokkaido University. Worked as a journalist in Boston, U.S.A. Moved to Yakushima in 1994. Serves as Director of NPO Yakushima Eco Festa. Writing books about Yakushima and historical events in Japan and how they relate to the western world and the present. Since 2011 researching the life, work and writings of Ernest Henry Wilson.

著書／ Chief Literary Works:

（日本語　Japanese）『夢みる旅「赤毛のアン」』（文藝春秋）『屋久島恋泊日記』（南日本新聞社）『屋久島　島・ひと・昔語り』（南日本開発センター）『密行 最後の伴天連シドッティ』（新人物往来社）『はじまりのかたち- 屋久島民具ものがたり』（NPO法人屋久島エコ・フェスタ）など
（日本語・英語 Japanese & English）『ウィルソンの屋久島-100年の記憶の旅路』（KTC中央出版、2014年度南日本出版文化賞受賞）"Wilson's Yakushima- Memories of the Past"＜Awarded Best Book in Southern Japan,2014＞『ウィルソンが見た鹿児島-プラント・ハンターの足跡を追って』（南方新社）"Wilson's Kagoshima- Tracing the Footsteps of a Plant Hunter"
（伊語 Italian）『L'ultimo missionario La storia segreta di Giovanni Battista Sidotti in Giappone』（Terra Santa srl）

Wilson in Okinawa
ウィルソン　沖縄の旅　1917

2017年9月7日　初版第1刷発行
2018年6月7日　第2刷発行

著　者　古居智子
発行者　富田詢一
発行所　琉球新報社
　　　　〒900－8525
　　　　沖縄県那覇市泉崎1－10－3
問合せ　琉球新報社読者事業局出版部
　　　　電話（098）865－5100
発　売　琉球プロジェクト
印刷所　新星出版株式会社

Ⓒ Tomoko Furui 2017 Printed in Japan
ISBN978-4-89742-225-1 C0072
定価はカバーに表示してあります。
万一、落丁・乱丁の場合はお取り替えいたします。
※本書の無断使用を禁じます。